Total Quality Management

**Marshall Sashkin
and
Kenneth J. Kiser**

Ducochon Press   **Seabrook Maryland**

ISBN 0-9630714-0-8

Library of Congress Catalog Card Number: 91-92982

Printed in the United States of America
by International Graphics, Inc.,
Brentwood, Maryland.

Third printing, revised, 1992.

Technical Advisor: Ken Jones.

Production Coordinator: Molly G. Sashkin.

Cover design by Milt Feinstein, Inc., Graphic
Design and Production.

Illustrations prepared by Richard L. Williams,
with the assistance of Paul Rossler.

Ducochon Press logo created by Stephen C. Ogden.

Contents

Preface

Introduction 1

Chapter One: What is TQM? 5

Chapter Two: TQM Tools and Techniques 37

Chapter Three: Quality for the Customer 45

Chapter Four: The Cultural Basis of TQM 59

Chapter Five: Creating and Leading a TQM Culture 87

Chapter Six: What Does the Future Hold? 111

Notes 121

Appendix A: The Seven Old Tools 151

Appendix B: The Baldrige Award 159

Appendix C: Resources 169

Index 175

Preface

This short book started out as a much shorter paper. Both of us deal with managers in various educational and consulting situations. Over the past year or two we found an increasing number of managers asking questions or making assertions about "total quality management." There seemed to be a real need for a brief document that would, in a clear and straightforward manner, describe this concept, answer the most frequently-asked questions, and correct the most common misconceptions. Thus, we started to write such a brief article. However, before we knew it, our brief article had grown beyond the bounds of a ten or twenty-page handout. So we refocused our efforts on a short monograph. But, again, the monograph got out of hand; we found ourselves with a manuscript that was definitely book-length.

As is always the case in writing, whether it be a paper or a book, we learned a great deal. Exploring a concept, we sometimes found our initial understanding to be off-target. More often, we saw that our views were incomplete, that a fuller and sometimes significantly more complex perspective was required to really understand what we had thought to be a relatively simple point.

This posed a dilemma for us. Were we to follow the lines of inquiry to the end, we would have a very different book than the one we wanted to write. Our product would address the scholar or someone with deep practical experience, not the inquiring and interested manager who was not an expert. We solved our problem by writing at two levels. The first level is directed toward our primary audience — the practicing manager. We assume no particular background or knowledge, just a need to know about total quality management in a clear and practically–relevant way.

But we also provide a variety of fine details and more technically sophisticated discussions as endnotes that are referenced consecutively throughout the text. We needed these notes partly because, as scholars, we are committed to full and complete citation of all of the sources of information we use. But we also took advantage of this necessity, by using the notes to elaborate and discuss a number of issues, some minor and some fairly significant. Both the scholar and the very knowledgeable practitioner should find interesting at least some of the concerns raised in these endnotes.

It may seem to someone unfamiliar with total quality management that there is considerable agreement among those who research and implement this approach. In fact, there is considerable *dis*agreement with respect to approaches to total quality management. One may be a "Juran person," a "Deming acolyte," a "Crosby devotee," or a follower of any of a dozen other "gurus" in the field of total quality management. We have tried to give a relatively balanced treatment of the various "personalities" involved in total quality management, but we do have some biases and you will find them easy to identify. Even if we do not seem to follow your own favorite approach, you may still find that we have managed to incorporate the most important elements into our own view.

We received a great deal of help from students, colleagues, and friends. Despite a relatively sound knowledge of the field and its literature, we could never have produced this document without the extensive assistance of many people. To those who made special efforts, we want to express our deepest appreciation and gratitude.

Richard L. Williams prepared the illustrations in Chapter One and Appendix A, and commented in detail on early drafts of the manuscript. Paul Rossler read and made extensive notes on almost every page of an early draft, often pushing us gently in the right direction. He also designed the control chart we use as an example. Gregory Boudreaux provided crucial strategic advice, helped us refine and clarify our concepts of how TQM becomes part of organizational operations, and gave many valuable editorial suggestions as well. The positive influence he has had on this final product is very great. In terms of both general direction and specific detail, his efforts are visible throughout the book.

Robert M. Fulmer also provided advice of extraordinary quality; he was especially helpful in guiding us to see and improve the flow and organization of the material. Terrence Deal reviewed and responded to our discussions of culture and culture change with specific suggestions, most of which we followed. We hope that his deep knowledge of organizational culture and its shaping is reflected in our work. By sharing his disagreements, Erich Prien helped us sharpen (and, occasionally, temper) our arguments. We were fortunate to be able to tap into Paul Tolchinsky's vast knowledge of total quality management in the U.S. and Japan. Muriel Converse helped us strengthen our descriptions of the TQM culture–building processes described in Chapter Five. Denise Rousseau is a scholar who pressed us to focus on practical applications. Kenneth Blanchard encouraged us both directly and by his leadership model. Finally, we thank Warren Bennis, whose inspiration proved invaluable. His concepts and writings on organizations and leadership are incorporated throughout this book.

We are also grateful to those of our colleagues in organizations who read and reviewed our drafts, especially CarolAnn Auclair and William H. Clover. Brigette Nix provided extensive and detailed feedback (both her own and her colleagues') on more than one draft. The results of her efforts to get us to address union issues and concerns are evident in Chapter Five and greatly improved the final draft. Special thanks are due Eva Pang, whose masters thesis, "Developing a Quality Improvement Taxonomy," proved to be a treasure trove of definitions, explications, and references. While we took no single thing or quote from it that appears directly in this book, we recognize our debt to her for doing some of the hardest background work.

Throughout the book we have relied on facts reported in David Halberstam's fascinating book, *The Reckoning,* as well as on Mary Walton's marvelously clear presentation of the ideas of W. Edwards Deming, in her book *The Deming Management Method.* To both of these authors we extend our thanks as well as our admiration.

We must also acknowledge the pioneering efforts of those who defined and created the practice of total quality management, especially Walter A. Shewhart, W. Edwards Deming, and Joseph M. Juran. If not for them and those who followed their early lead there would be no TQM to write about.

Despite our deep debts to the individuals named above, along with other colleagues whose earlier work was the foundation for our own, this book — and any flaws or errors it may include — is strictly our responsibility and any blame remains ours alone. Moreover, we do not mean to suggest that the persons named above would necessarily agree with any specific point we make.

Of course, we owe the most (and sometimes give the least) to our families, especially Molly Sashkin, who was deeply involved in the book's design and who coordinated all aspects of its technical production, and Pamela Peevy–Kiser.

We hope that this book proves useful to you. We are very concerned about the fate of America in the twenty-first century. Like many others who have studied the issues dealt with here, David Halberstam believes, as stated in his book, *The Next Century,* that the post-millenium world will find its center in the Pacific, not Washington or any of the (formerly) great industrial cities of the U.S. We agree, in general, but we also believe that it is not yet decided whether America will share in creating the twenty-first century or will be frozen out and forced to live in the past, on remembered achievements. The choice is not a matter of fate or fortune; it is up to us. The ideas in this book are absolutely crucial if we hope to enter the next century as serious players in a "New World Order."

Introduction

In American business and industry, even in government and public service agencies, the watchword these days is "quality," often heard as "total quality" or "total quality management." We will call it "TQM," for short. But what *is* TQM, and where did it come from? How does it work? How can an organization adopt a TQM approach? These are some of the questions we will address.

To put it simply, this book addresses three factors that are important foundations of TQM. The first concerns "tools" and techniques that people are trained to use to identify and solve quality problems. The second factor centers on the customer as the focus of TQM. The third foundation is the organization's culture. A TQM culture is based on certain values and leadership vision.

In the first chapter we take up the question of defining Total Quality Management. This is not as easy as it might seem. To understand just what TQM is we must first provide some historical background. Then, we must distinguish TQM from related terms, such as "Quality Circles," and disentangle TQM from factors (such as "self-managing teams") that are connected to TQM only indirectly.

Next, we look at the "inner workings" of TQM, at least those that are most commonly seen and understood. These are the tools and techniques that organization members learn to apply to identify and solve quality problems. However, important as tools, techniques, and training are, they are only the superficial evidence of TQM. Effective implementation of TQM calls for much more than training people to use certain tools and techniques.

In Chapter Three we uncover the first real hint of what really makes TQM work. What's needed is an all–encompassing determination to meet customer and client needs and deliver quality for the customer. Doing this requires a systemic, organizational understanding of TQM. We must go well beyond tools and techniques to see how TQM can become an integral part of the organization's operating systems. Even this is not the complete answer; there is still more to TQM.

We turn next to the deepest level of TQM: organizational culture and transformation. The new, TQM culture is what supports the driving aim of quality for the customer. To reach this aim certain values and beliefs must become part of the organization's culture.

These values include, of course, the overriding importance of quality. But the values and beliefs needed to support TQM extend far beyond a simple belief in the importance of quality. They deal with what Rensis Likert called "the human organization,"[1] that is, with the way people believe they should be treated and with the things they value in the organization. We will examine some value issues of special importance for TQM. These include the basis for rewards, the relationship that should exist between authority and responsibility, and the way people believe they should work together.

We will then look at how to create and construct organizational cultures, and especially at the role leaders must play to develop and support a TQM culture. We also examine the role of unions in TQM. In our concluding chapter we discuss how the issues dealt with in this book are being played out in real-world organizations and what the future might hold for TQM.

In sum, there are three important aspects of TQM:

- *counting* — tools, techniques, and training in their use for analyzing, understanding, and solving quality problems;

- *customers* — quality for the customer as a driving force and central concern; and,

- *culture* — shared values and beliefs, expressed by leaders, that define and support quality.

If all this seems more difficult than you had expected, you are right, it is. But if it seems impossible, then you are wrong. The "impossible" has been and is being done, and not just in Japan. In our review and explanation we will give real examples of American firms, large and small, that have successfully applied TQM. Only then will it be fair to close with some answers to the question of whether striving for TQM represents a realistic goal.

While our focus is practical, this book is not a "how to" guide to TQM. In the final chapter we will outline a few important first steps that you can take to begin the process of total quality management in your organization. We will not, however, try to explain how to implement each of the many specific programs, policies and actions that make up a comprehensive approach to TQM. There are many good books and resources to help in applying one or another of these TQM elements. We will identify some of the most useful resources throughtout this book, as well as in Appendix C, a brief "practical guide" at the end.

In this short book our aim is modest. We propose to help you understand what TQM really is, apart from all the hoopla and hurrahs. Then, you can decide whether TQM is "right" for you. If you conclude that TQM should be part of your own organization, then the first steps to take will be clear and you will also understand — and be able to avoid — the major traps and pitfalls in moving to TQM.

Our own bias is no secret: we believe that unless many more American organizations follow the TQM path, America will enter the new millennium as a second-rate competitor headed downhill. We do not see this as inevitable. There are choices to be made, important ones. Our purpose is to help you make the right choice.

Chapter One

What is TQM?

The term "total quality management" means different things to different people. Our aim in this chapter is to arrive at a common understanding of TQM, highlighting those elements or aspects shared by most or all definitions. We begin by examining where TQM came from.

It all started with a Japanese "import" called quality circles (or quality control circles). At least, that's what first caught American managers' attention. We will refer to this technique as "QCs." The idea behind QCs is to have workers meet occasionally, for an hour or so each week, to discuss work problems. As a result of their discussion the workers develop ideas about how to solve the problems they have identified.

QCs became popular in Japan during the 1960s and 70s. Beginning formally in 1962, by 1980 there were over 100,000 QCs in operation in Japanese organizations of all types. Workers who were part of a "team" would meet around a table at a regular time during the week, usually before or after working hours. The team members would discuss problems, usually problems that concerned the quality of production. Based on these discussions they would develop solutions and pass these ideas on to management. The aim was usually improved product quality; that's how the technique got its name, "quality circles."

American firms began using QCs in the mid–1970s; they gained in popularity throughout the 1980s. By 1986 QCs were so common that **Business Week** included them as a fad of the 80s.[2] The story also noted that QCs seemed to have mixed results. Not every QC "installation" was a grand success, as you will see from the following real–life case.

A QC Installation Example:
Graft the Leg from the Donkey

In 1980 the management of the admissions office at a large east–coast university decided to start a Quality Circles program. After sixteen months management canceled the project, which was an obvious failure. This occurred even though management had initially been enthusiastic and had hired a reputable consultant to do the installation.

The twenty people in the office were assigned at random to meet in QC groups of four persons each. Since everyone did essentially the same job there was no other logical basis for forming groups.

The groups met after work, at lunch, or on "break time." As is usual with a QC, the topics were to be work–related concerns and problems, with a view toward possible solutions. While they lacked formal QC training, all employees were college graduates who saw themselves as professionals. Managers apparently felt that their basic group discussion skills were adequate and that no special QC training was needed.

Over the sixteen months during which the QCs operated they discussed many problems but resolved few. After a time some participants complained to management that the meetings often degenerated into "gripe sessions." Moreover, it seemed that those doing the most complaining were interested in doing the least work. Some workers reported that the most frequently–discussed "problem" was how to get away with doing as little work as possible!

After about ten months there were some changes in management; the new managers were much less supportive of or interested in the QC program. When the facts noted above became evident to these new managers, they abolished it.

Why did this effort fail? Would training have helped the new technique to succeed? Probably not. It is not really that hard to understand this failure. To sum it up, the organizational culture in which these employees worked was very different from that of the typical Japanese firm involved with QCs.

Rather than a history of loyalty of employees to the organization, based on trust and support, there was a history of acrimony and deception. Rather than a shared sense of purpose and problems, there were strong differences in how employees and managers defined both the purposes and problems of the organization.

The employees thought of themselves as professionals. They defined the job as first determining whether potential applicants to the college should be admitted. For those who should, the next step was providing academic counseling.

However, despite their college–level training, management did not treat these employees as professionals. Instead, managers saw them as clerks or low–level technical staff. They received wages much lower than did persons with comparable training and experience who were working in business or industry. And they were subject to controls more commonly applied to hourly than to salaried employees.

While they saw themselves as professional admissions counselors, managers saw these employees as salespersons whose primary task was to market the college to acceptable applicants. The sole criterion for acceptance was the Scholastic Aptitude Test score; anyone scoring above a certain point would be admitted, at least provisionally. Thus, managers neither expected nor permitted much actual academic advising. Employees were even given "pitches" to follow when attempting to "sign up" acceptable potential students.

Employees defined their job as identifying applicants' needs and interests and then guiding them into the right programs. Managers defined the work aim as increasing the number of acceptable applicants who actually enrolled. The issues that managers wanted the QCs to deal with were different from the work–relevant problems defined by employees.

In sum, the cultural support that permits QCs to be just another expression of the underlying social and cultural solidarity of the Japanese organization was simply absent. No sense of meaningful purpose existed, binding together individuals and groups to achieve the organization's goals.

Our failed example of the admissions office involved the application of a technique — quality circles — with neither a client–centered purpose nor a systemic organizational commitment to quality improvement. To put it as cynically as some employees, management's only real aim was to squeeze more productivity out of employees. Employees who saw the situation this way refused to cooperate; when managers realized this they ended the program.

Throughout the 1980s it became obvious that all too many QC "installations" were suffering some variation of the fate just described. In one West Virginia manufacturing plant QCs were installed in 1981 but failed dismally — after the company laid off half its employees.[3]

These and other failures of QCs were probably due more to the way the approach was used than to some flaw with the technique. That is, it has been common practice for "QC trainers" to offer and provide services to "install" QCs. This treats QCs as something that can be bolted on to an organization, like an afterburner that has been attached to a factory furnace to provide cleaner emissions. W. Edwards Deming, a major force in the movement toward TQM has said, "A usual stumbling block [in quality improvement efforts] . . . is management's supposition that quality control is something that you install, like . . . a new carpet."[4]

The effect is like trying to graft a fifth leg from a donkey onto an overweight cow, to help the cow support her weight. An interesting idea, but sure to be rejected in the end — though not, perhaps, before the managers involved receive a few solid kicks of the donkey's leg, before it is rejected by the corporate body.

The quality circle technique is best used in the context of an organization-wide quality improvement effort. Used that way, in an organizational culture designed to support TQM, quality circles can be useful and productive. But QCs represent a technique that came later, not a defining attribute of TQM. In Japan the total quality movement started in the late 1940s and was in full swing by 1960. The first QC in Japan, however, was not formed until 1962. It was not until the mid-1970s that QCs were widespread in Japan — and being introduced (or re-introduced) in America.

QCs: The "Made In America" Import

If QCs developed to suit the Japanese organizational culture, it would be understandable that their implementation in American organizations might be problematic. The technique, however, was not really new. It was in the 1940s that American industrial consultants — in a mens' shirt and pajama factory — first got groups of workers to talk over and try to solve their everyday work problems.[5] Some of the consultants' associates went on to apply this technique in other organizations. A variety of American organizations used this group problem-solving approach over the next twenty-five years.[6] However, the approach did not become popular until, after a quarter-century, it was reintroduced as an "exotic" Japanese management technique!

Is there evidence that quality circles really work, that they really improve production quality? The answer must be a *qualified* yes. That is, QCs typically start out heralded as a major new quality improvement approach, and they often appear to deliver results, at least at first. But after the initial enthusiasm fades it often becomes clear that nothing has really changed. Eventually, both workers and managers lose interest in QCs. In many organizations QCs just "fade away" within a year or two.

After failures like those just described, consultants as well as managers began to see that for QCs to "take root" and make a long-term difference more is needed than a room with table and chairs and an hour a week overtime pay for the workers. It was about this time that American management "discovered" the field of *quality improvement* (which has now become so popular that it has all but replaced earlier concerns with *productivity* improvement).

This discovery came in two stages. First, it became obvious that if one wanted a quality product one looked to Japanese, not American manufacturers. That is one reason for the fad–like initial popularity of QCs; managers thought, "Maybe this is the Japanese 'secret'!" However, as we have explained, people eventually realized that whatever the merit of QCs, this was not the secret behind Japan's success.

In looking more closely at the "why" and "how" of Japanese quality, American managers stumbled across a more important part of the "secret:" an *American* industrial consultant. Perhaps this first caught peoples' attention when Japanese firms like Matsushita (Panasonic) "bragged" (quietly, of course) about winning "the Deming Prize." (Today Cadillac advertisements now brag — more openly — about winning the Malcolm Baldrige National Quality Award.)[7]

The Remarkable Dr. Deming

W. Edwards Deming began his career as an industrial engineer investigating problems of quality control. Working at the Hawthorne plant of AT&T's subsidiary firm, Western Electric, Deming observed the production of switching equipment and other telephone–related hardware.[8] He quickly realized that the traditional practice of inspecting products and sorting out those with defects, to be corrected later, was both foolish and costly. He pointed out that quality is not improved by inspection after the fact but by control over the production process as it happens. Deming saw that workers were the only parties who could, and had to, exercise such control. The problem was that the typical worker had neither the latitude nor the skills needed to do so.

In the early 1920s Western Electric created a new department, to study the problem of quality and its control. Deming learned first hand of the groundbreaking work of a key member of this group, an engineer named Walter A. Shewhart. It was Shewhart who first recognized the importance of understanding and measuring the *variability* of a product's dimensions and attributes. Then one can seek out the causes of variations beyond acceptable limits. Finally, one can take actions and make changes to reduce variability or bring it within the acceptable range.[9] Shewhart devised statistical techniques for making these types of measurements. He also invented ways to display the results in easy–to–follow graphs.

After he received his doctorate in physics from Yale, Deming rejected a job offer from Bell Labs. Instead he accepted a position with the U.S. Department of Agriculture. But he travelled frequently to New Jersey to study with Shewhart, who was then leading a research group at Bell Labs.

In the 1930s and 40s, working with Shewhart and on his own, Deming refined and improved on Shewhart's ideas and tools. He modified Shewhart's "specification–production–inspection" cycle of quality control activity, inventing what is now known as the Deming Cycle (plan–do–check–act). He even improved some statistical methods first developed by Shewhart, publishing his results as papers and reports in various professional journals.

Deming also spent a great deal of his time teaching others to use the quality control tools and techniques he had learned, modified, or invented. Deming taught engineers, technicians, and ordinary employees how to make project timeline (or "Gantt") charts. He showed them how to take random samples of output and then plot the variability of important characteristics on "statistical control charts."

The Control Chart: Deming's Crucial Tool

The single tool most associated with Deming and his "statistical process control" approach is the control chart (Figure 1). A control chart is a graphic display of measurements of an important product or process variable. In a manufacturing situation an example might be the diameter of a ball bearing. In a service context, the measure might be the presence or absence on an insurance claim form of certain required information. The measure is taken at different times, using a statistical sampling procedure. The control chart displays these results, over time. The chart shows the upper and lower extremes of a "normal" distribution, so that one can see whether the actual measures fall within the statistically–defined limits of such a distribution.

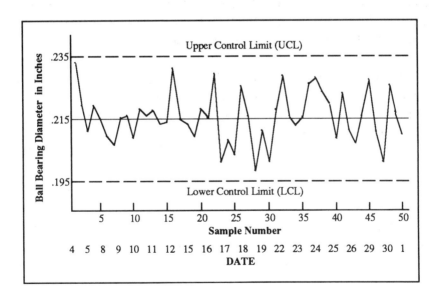

Figure 1: A Control Chart

Assuming a normal distribution, most of the measures will be close to, but somewhat different from the overall mean or average; few things are ever exactly "average." The typical or average difference of the random measures from the overall mean is called the "standard deviation." The standard deviation tells you how variable a measurement is. If the measures form a normal distribution, then over 99% will fall somewhere between plus three and minus three standard deviations from the mean. That is, we would almost never find a case of a measure so high, so far above the mean, as to be more than three times the average difference from the mean. Nor would we expect to obtain a measure so low as to be below the mean by more than three times the average difference from the mean. So, plus–three standard deviations is referred to as the "upper control limit" or UCL while minus–three standard deviations is called the "lower control limit" or LCL. The UCL and LCL can be calculated, approximately, by knowing the average, the range, and the number of measures made.

Every control chart shows the UCL and LCL, so one can easily see whether the actual measures ever (or usually) exceed the UCL or go below the LCL. (This means that before using this "statistical tool" for quality control, one must obtain sample measures to get an average and range. Then one can calculate the UCL and LCL, based on an estimate of variability and assuming a normal distribution.) When measures on the control chart are above the UCL or below the LCL, the process is "out of control." Through careful study one can find out what is wrong and determine how to correct it. Having a record of sample measures at different times helps a great deal, since one then knows at just what point in time to look for problems.

Consider our ball bearing. One would take random samples of, say, the diameter of the ball bearings produced. The data would be used to calculate the UCL and LCL of a control chart. From then on, a control chart could be used to track the production process. Samples would be taken at specific times, for example, every three hours. The data are plotted on the control chart, with the diameter on the vertical axis and time along the horizontal. All is well if the measurements all fall within the upper and lower control limits.

What if some ball bearings have a diameter greater than the UCL or smaller than the LCL? This means some ball bearings are so large or so small they would not be found if the actual distribution of sizes forms a normal, bell–shaped curve. Thus, the distribution is not normal. And that, in turn, means that the process is not in control; something is wrong and must be corrected.

One usually isn't satisfied just to have the variability fall within the UCL and LCL. Generally, the measurement tolerances allowed for a product or service — the specifications — will be "tighter" than just plus or minus three standard deviations. The maximum desired measure will be below the UCL and the lowest acceptable measure above the LCL. These "specification limits" may appear on the control chart, as lines placed below the UCL and above the LCL. Once a process is "in control" one looks not just for samples above the UCL or below the LCL, but for samples that fall outside the specification limits. But constant improvement of quality does not simply mean producing within certain limits. The work process must be studied and improved so that variability is made less and less. This is the only way to consistently reach a specific, desired product or service measure and thus increase the level of quality.

The issue at the heart of quality control is understanding the variability in key or crucial measures of a product (or service). First one controls that variability, so it stays within certain, specified limits. Then, one works to narrow those limits, to reduce variability still further. When the distribution is normal, that is, bell–shaped, it is safe to assume that there are no unknown outside factors affecting variability. If there were, the distribution would appear tilted or "skewed" in one way or another. When the measures that make up the distribution are all within specifications, then the process is in control. If the distribution is not bell–shaped (this can be determined by using statistical tools) or if some sample measures fall outside the specifications shown on the control chart, one must find and correct the cause of the undesired variation.

The cause might be something done, not done, or done incorrectly by a worker. Deming refers to these as "special causes." However (and, according to Deming, far more likely), the cause might instead be due to problems with the raw materials, problems with the manufacturing process, or problems with the service plan. These problem sources are attributable to or the responsibility of management, not workers. Deming calls them "common causes." No matter how "motivated" workers may be to do a good job, problems caused by the system cannot be corrected by telling employees to "do better," by rewarding them for better results, or even by punishing them for undesirable outcomes.

Deming points out that managers often assume that employees' actions are the cause of problems (like too many oversized ball bearings). He believes, however, that such assumptions are usually wrong, that the real causes are typically beyond employees' control. Deming argues that the underlying causes of most quality problems are the responsibility of management, especially top management, not employees.

It is management that designed and maintains in operation the systems that cause the problems. When a work process, such as the making of ball bearings, is out of control due to bad raw materials or defects in one or another machine, workers cannot be blamed for the poor quality of the output. Nor do they generally have the authority to take action to correct the problem.[10]

But this takes us beyond a description of the control chart to a concern with its use, in the context of TQM. We will return to the issue of how and by whom control charts and other tools and techniques are used. Here, we have considered the nature and aims of this tool.

To sum up, control charts have three purposes. First, they help one to describe and understand a work activity, a "process." This is a matter of counting, recording, and interpreting the results. Second, control charts tell when the data do not fit a normal distribution, that is, a bell-shaped curve. This is important, because it helps one to focus on, understand, and correct the causes of such abnormal variation. Moreover, it also becomes possible to "tighten up" this distribution, to make output even less variable. Third, control charts provide information needed to think about changing and improving work processes, so that higher levels of quality can be achieved. This is what continuous improvement is about, in terms of statistical process control.

Training People to Apply the Tools: The Answer?

Control charts, quality control circles, and all the other tools and techniques we will describe have the same aim: helping people to track and then control variability in manufacturing or service processes. It might, then, seem that training people to use these tools will lead to TQM. Many organizations have taken just this approach.

In the mid–1980s a small manufacturer in the midwest, supplying parts to the auto industry, decided to apply statistical process control (SPC) techniques throughout the organization to improve quality. Working with a local college, and with some special support from a state job skills development program, human resources department staff developed and implemented a plan for training all employees in SPC.

First, top managers attended an introductory seminar. Next, technical, supervisory, and managerial employees went through a series of short training sessions to learn how to use the basic tools, including control charts. The technical personnel received additional training in applying some more sophisticated tools to solve quality problems. Finally, a group of internal trainers learned how to teach employees and managers to use the basic SPC tools, so that new employees could be trained and refresher courses could be given.

The training program ended after about four months and, for a time, the results seemed positive. During the second year, however, there was less use of the tools, both by lower–level employees on the line and by the more technically–qualified staff. Managers, especially at the top, became less and less involved in the on–going SPC program. Top management support, more a matter of encouragement than active involvement from the start of the project, became less evident.

Today there are still individuals in this firm who use one or another of the basic tools; many of the more senior technical personnel report that they sometimes use certain advanced tools. However, there is nothing that one could call a coherent program, focused on quality control or quality improvement.

The experience of this firm has been repeated many times. A company acts on its commitment to training, people learn to apply various tools and techniques, and everything looks great — for a while. But use of tools and techniques then drops off; people go back to the "old ways," or just don't bother to go to the trouble of making and maintaining control charts. Why, we must ask, does this happen?

Why Do Tools Fail?

Our example, though it happened in the 1980s, merely repeats Deming's experience almost a half–century earlier. That is, during the 1930s and 40s Deming's teachings (as well as Shewhart's ideas and those of other quality control consultants) were widely adopted by American industry. Deming found himself training group after group of workers, supervisors, and engineers, in his quality control methods.

In the 1940s Deming took a new assignment with the Federal Government, applying his methods to national measurement problems, focusing on industrial production for the war effort. Again, he had many successes. Chronicling the decline of the American automobile industry in his book *The Reckoning,* David Halberstam points out how during the war Japanese engineers would examine captured American military equipment and marvel at its quality. It was then that they first realized, according to Halberstam, just how hopelessly outmatched they were.

After the war, when Deming returned to industrial consulting in American organizations, he was surprised to find no one using his methods; hardly anyone even remembered them! For a while he tried to teach the methods to a new generation of workers and engineers, but his efforts had little lasting impact. The workers and engineers were interested, but their managers didn't seem to care.

American management was riding the postwar boom, with an undemanding and apparently inexhaustible supply of consumers who wanted products, after years of wartime scarcity. Quality did not seem to be important to them. Deming realized that despite all his work before the war he had made no lasting impression on the organizations he had worked with because he had made no impression on management. He took a position with the Bureau of the Census, as a statistical sampling expert.

If Not America, Why Not Japan?

It was in the late 40s that the Bureau sent Deming to Japan to help the post–war Japanese government improve its census capability. Deming made contact with industrial engineers, too. In 1950, still generally ignored by American industry, he returned to Japan at the invitation of a new professional organization of engineers and scientists.

The founders of this organization, the Japan Union of Scientists and Engineers (JUSE), were concerned with the very poor quality of Japanese products. They intended to change this situation. Deming agreed to help with a lecture tour, talking to large groups of technicians, researchers, engineers, and plant managers.

In her book on *The Deming Management Method,* Mary Walton reports that in the middle of his first lecture Deming had a sense of déjà vu. He realized that if he simply lectured and taught engineers and technicians his methods, the same thing as had happened in America would happen in Japan. That is, when consumer demand grew, management would abandon his methods and focus only on production at the expense of quality.

This realization led Deming to see if he could get to the "right people," the top executives of Japanese organizations. One of those on the committee that had invited Deming, Ichiro Ishikawa, was a former professor of many such top executives. Ishikawa was also head of Keidanren, the Japanese Federation of Economic Organizations, Japan's most prestigious and powerful organization of business leaders. Deming knew nothing of this; he simply asked his host, Ishikawa, whether it might be possible to arrange a special session with a group of top industrial managers.

In *The Reckoning* Halberstam tells how Ishikawa cabled top Japanese industrial leaders, inviting them to attend Deming's lecture. Coming from Ishikawa, that invitation had the effect of an order; every one of them showed up. Two more meetings with almost a hundred other top managers followed — all in addition to the lectures that Deming gave for thousands of technical personnel.

Unlike American management, Japanese top managers paid attention to Deming. They went to work with a passion; they knew they had to rebuild their industrial base if Japan was to prosper in the coming years. They were well aware of Japan's reputation for inferior quality. To become a real competitor in the world economy Japan had to change and improve.

The Japanese top managers applied Deming's lessons rigorously, throughout their organizations; they truly took to heart Deming's teachings. At first some, perhaps many, did not really believe that Deming's methods would work. They applied them anyway, to avoid losing face by disobeying this American expert, sent by the U.S. government to help them.[11]

Throughout the 1950s Japanese firms vied among themselves to see which could go the farthest in applying Deming's ideas. They quickly established an all–industry competition and an annual prize for the organization that demonstrated the most comprehensive and effective applications. In Japan teachers are honored and respected, so they named the prize after their first and most important teacher, W. Edwards Deming.[12]

Deming was a good student as well as a teacher.[13] He learned from his disappointing experiences after the war that it was not simply the use of one or another tool aimed at quality improvement that was crucial for achieving quality. Only management's commitment produced quality. Later, Deming observed, ". . . no permanent impact has ever been accomplished in quality control without [the] understanding and nurture of top management."[14]

The Japanese proved that Deming had learned the right lesson. They went far beyond application of this or that tool; in fact, they invented or adopted many new tools, some that were much more sophisticated than those given them by Deming. But they never lost sight of the end, the aim, the purpose for using the tool. That purpose was to produce the level of quality of either goods or services that customers wanted.

Was It Deming Or Was It Japan?

Deming was not the only American consultant to go teach the Japanese about how to improve their manufacturing base. He was not even the only one to receive the Order of the Sacred Treasure (Second Rank) from the Emperor; he shares that honor with another well–known quality consultant, Dr. Joseph M. Juran.

Juran first went to Japan several years after Deming, but he made the same sort of lecture/consulting tours. Many years later, Juran was asked whether it was true that he and Deming had been the key forces behind Japan's post–war turnaround. Some people in the West, Juran replied, think

> the Japanese miracle was . . . due to two Americans, Deming and Juran, who lectured to the Japanese soon after World War II. Deming will have to speak for himself. As for Juran, I am agreeably flattered but I regard the conclusion as ludicrous. I did indeed lecture in Japan as reported, and I did bring something new to them — a structured approach to quality. I also did the same thing for a great many other countries, yet none of these attained the results achieved by the Japanese. So who performed the miracle?[15]

In *The Reckoning* Halberstam emphasizes Deming's role. Even so, he observes that right after the war (and before Deming appeared) there was a small group of key Japanese industrial leaders who had already concluded that Japanese manufacturers had to change radically if Japan was to aspire again to industrial greatness. They recognized that this change had to emphasize not just productivity but quality, as well. Some of these men were the very ones who had laboriously translated the early work of Shewhart into Japanese — and who had invited Deming and other quality consultants to come to Japan to teach them about quality improvement.

There is an even more basic — and less obvious — factor that helped Japanese companies to focus quickly and successfully on the aim of customer and client quality satisfaction. This factor comes into play because Japanese organizations are far more homogenous and cohesive than firms in many other countries.

The cultural cohesiveness and strength characteristic of Japanese organizations reflect the cultural homogeneity of Japanese society. Visitors who have been in Japan for any length of time know the experience of being treated as "gaijin," outsiders. There is little room in the Japanese culture for outsiders; at best, one is politely tolerated. At worst, one is openly ostracized.

In developing a societal commitment to rebuilding their industry on the basis of quality and customer satisfaction, the Japanese had the advantage of a strong social culture. In developing an organizational commitment to quality, Japanese firms started with a similar advantage due to strong and cohesive *organizational* cultures.

The observations of Halberstam and of Juran lead to the same conclusion. That is, in Japan it was possible for top–level industrial leaders to consciously decide to pursue quality with the greatest possible effort and to do so consistently, across industries. It was not long after the war that MITI, the powerful Ministry of International Trade and Industry, made this aim explicit.

Certainly Deming, Juran, and a relatively small number of others (including Ichiro Ishikawa and his son, Kaoru[16]) were key players in the dramatic revitalization of Japanese industry. But to suggest that they were the primary cause would be missing the point. TQM depends not on consultants or techniques but upon making the strongest possible commitment to quality improvement.

A Definition

We can now see that TQM is not quality circles, statistical process control, or any of the other tools developed and taught by Deming and others, although such tools are necessary.

Quality control is defined by Japanese Industrial Standard Z8101–1981,[17] as

> a system of means to economically produce goods or services which satisfy customers' requirements.

This "standard" goes beyond the notion of tools to incorporate a more sophisticated understanding of TQM. This new concept has two parts. First, it refers to "a system of means," or tools. That is, the tools are used systematically, as a coherent and integrated approach. Second, this definition centers on the pervasive and persistent focus on customers and what they want. This simple standard makes it clear that quality is much more than a collection of tools and techniques.

But Japanese Industrial Standard Z8101–1981 still does not give us a complete definition of TQM. Yes, TQM does incorporate a very strong focus on customers and a coherent, integrated approach to quality, but that is neither an adequate definition nor an accurate explanation for the success of Japanese firms in using TQM.

As Deming discovered, successful TQM requires that the focus on customer satisfaction through quality must be built into the management processes of the organization. That is, the very "fabric" of organizational life, the organization's culture, must define and support TQM. Thus,

> *TQM means that the organization's culture is defined by and supports the constant attainment of customer satisfaction through an integrated system of tools, techniques, and training. This involves the continuous improvement of organizational processes, resulting in high quality products and services.*

For TQM to work, certain tools will be needed, tools that most American organizations use poorly if at all. For TQM to succeed, management must believe in and act to achieve quality for customers and clients as a primary organizational aim. But the underlying essence of TQM, the existence and definition of TQM, is using tools to achieve the aim of quality for customers by creating a *culture*, a pattern of shared values and beliefs. Culture supports the aim of quality for the customer and encourages the commitment of *all* organization members to that end.

Deming Again

Let us return, one more time, to W. Edwards Deming. We do so because unlike many other "quality experts," who remained focused on tools, techniques, and training, Deming became less concerned with these factors over time. Increasingly, Deming concentrated on TQM as a culture or, as he calls it, a philosophy of management.

Deming once was asked by a magazine interviewer why the Japanese had so successfully applied his teachings when American managers had not. In response, Deming said, "I think there is something fundamentally different [between Japanese and American business managers]. The best description I can think of is that the people have roots and the roots are the company."[18]

Over the forty years from 1950 to 1990 Deming came to focus more and more on his realization that management mattered even more than tools. He spoke somewhat less about control charts (though he never stopped teaching people how to use these and other tools) and began to talk more about *management* and the *philosophy* that management must develop and implement to achieve quality.[19] This new way of thinking is at the heart of his famous "fourteen points," and of his "seven deadly diseases" that afflict American management.

At different times Deming has referred to these as "principles," "obligations," and "points." Their number, too, has increased over the years. When we turn to the fourteen points, we quickly leave techno–jargon behind in favor of the management of culture. Consider Deming's points:[20]

1. *Create constancy of purpose for improvement of product and service.* Not only does Deming stress the need for a continuing emphasis on quality improvement, he also, more subtly, points out that profit should *not* be the primary purpose. Profit, for Deming, is a consequence, a by–product, of a management approach centered on quality.

2. *Adopt the new philosophy.* Here Deming reiterates the need for constancy of purpose, while emphasizing how important it is that it be shared, even inculcated like a philosophy (which it really is).

3. *Cease dependence on mass inspection.* Quality cannot be added on; it must be built in from the start. Mass inspec–tion is completely off the mark. It assumes that quality can be added on by correcting errors. Walton observes that this means workers are paid to make errors and are then paid again to correct them. This is not to say that workers like this any more than managers. Deming notes that almost all workers want to do work of high quality, work in which they can feel pride and a sense of accomplishment.

4. *End the practice of awarding business on price tag alone.* Deming does not advocate ignoring price when looking for

suppliers. He only insists that price is a relatively minor factor, especially compared with the supplier's interest in and willingness to meet the customer's needs — that is, the needs of the organization purchasing the supplies. (Those needs are, of course, driven in turn by the needs of the organization's clients and customers.)   Choice among suppliers should be based mostly on the quality of the materials they supply and their willingness to work to improve that quality, in the context of a long-term relationship.

Wal-Mart was known for years for its tough negotiating style with suppliers.   But, several years ago, CEO Sam Walton decided that poor relations with suppliers were hurting the company. He changed the strategy, to one of working with suppliers to develop new products that customers want and to improve the quality of production and delivery processes. This year Wal-Mart passed Sears as the nation's largest retailer.[21]

5.   *Improve constantly and forever the system of production and service.*   This restates management's never-ending obligation to seek out ways to improve quality. There is an interesting story told by one member of a team from an electronic controls manufacturer, formed to visit Motorola to study their exceptional system of production quality. The Motorola vice-president making a presentation showed the team a pager, one that was selling well on the Japanese market. He explained that the product had a "mean time between failures" of 100 years, and Motorola was working to extend this to 125 years. One team member said to the vice-president, "Excuse me, but isn't that just a little extreme?   After all, who would see a problem with an

MTBF of 100 years?" The vice–president gave the ques-
tioner a steely glare and said, "Constant improvement is
what we are all about."[22]

6. *Institute training.* Deming does not mean just training in
how to use statistical quality control and other tools for
improving quality, he means training in how to do the job.
Many workers never get adequate training in doing the jobs
for which they are responsible. In American industry about
70% of all training dollars go for management education
and development; only 30% is spent on training lower–
level line employees, those who actually make products or
deliver services. Not only can this lead to errors, it fosters
unclear understanding on the workers' parts of what
management expects of them. In Japan the proportions of
funds spent on training workers and managers are approximately the reverse. To make TQM work, front–line
employees must receive on–going training.

7. *Institute leadership.* Being a leader is different from being
a supervisor. Supervisors tell workers what to do and then
watch to make sure that they do it. They administer
rewards and discipline as needed to ensure that employees
comply with their orders. Leaders assume that workers
want to do the best job they can. At lower organizational
levels, the job of a leader is to assist workers, by coaching
and by arranging for training when needed. For top
management, leadership means designing the system on the
basis of TQM and applying strategic vision to build a TQM
culture.

8. *Drive out fear.* This is without a doubt one of the most
important of Deming's points. In many organizations

people are afraid to speak up, to point out problems, or even to just ask questions. In such organizations managers rule by fear, using either special favors or (more often) a variety of punishments to make sure that workers do as they are told. Sometimes people are even fired for bringing a problem to management's attention. A concern for quality requires that employees feel secure. High quality cannot be attained unless managers operate in a culture of openness, in which no one is afraid that telling the truth, pointing out a problem, or trying to learn to do the job better will lead to the loss of one's job.

9.   ***Break down barriers between staff areas.*** Traditional organizational structures encourage competition among units, departments, divisions, and so on. But this makes it difficult, if not impossible, to work together to achieve quality. People in different areas and departments must understand that they have the same overriding goals, that they are in competition with other organizations not with their colleagues and coworkers.

10.   ***Eliminate slogans, exhortations, and targets for the workforce.*** In this point Deming is criticizing those who think that quality can come from "motivation," from getting people all worked up through "motivational speakers" and inspirational tracts. This approach actually makes things worse, in the long run, because even if workers really want to do better they still don't know how, don't have the tools they need to improve, and are not supported by the organization's culture. Deming has said that slogans and targets put people in the position of having an idea of where they want to go but having no map of how to get there.

11. ***Eliminate numerical quotas.*** Quotas encourage people to ignore quality. The goal is to meet or exceed the quota, at any cost and regardless of quality. Mary Walton notes that inefficiency and high cost are also common outcomes when numerical quotas are stressed. Goals must focus on quality issues, not on numbers produced. (Recall the Motorola goal of a pager with an MTBF of 125 years.)

12. ***Remove barriers to pride of workmanship.*** Eliminate the annual rating or merit system. Deming assumes that people want to do a good job, not a poor one. They need help in overcoming barriers such as poor quality of the materials they receive to work with, poor quality of equipment, and inadequate job training. It does not help when people feel that they are being judged, ranked, and rated. The need is for a management–designed and supported system of operation that allows all employees to do their jobs well, rather than trying to coerce performance from them.

13. ***Institute a vigorous program of education and improvement.*** Deming does not downplay the need for everyone to have a sound grounding in quality control tools and techniques; these tools are the "language" of quality. But he also points out that people must learn new ways of working together, as teams, and new behaviors that support the new management philosophy — the TQM culture.

14. ***Take action to accomplish the transformation.*** Everyone in the organization must work together to implement a quality culture. Top management in particular must focus on a strategy and a plan, and must take actions to put the plan into effect. Workers cannot be expected to do it on their own, no matter how much training they receive in the

use of quality control tools and techniques. Only management can begin the process of getting the entire organization, management as well as workers, to take the actions
that result in a TQM culture.

These fourteen points are the basic elements of Deming's "new
philosophy," his "operational theory of management." Only when
these elements become an integral part of the organization's culture
is TQM in full operation.[23]

Deming is under no illusion about the difficulty of bringing this
new way of thinking to American organizations. To do so, he
asserts, means overcoming what he labels "the seven deadly
diseases." These are:

- Lack of constancy of purpose to improve products
  and services by providing resources for long-range
  planning, for research, and for training;

- An emphasis on short-term profits, and the quarterly dividend;

- Individual performance evaluations through merit
  ratings and annual reviews;

- Managers who are highly mobile, hopping from
  company to company;

- Use by management of numbers and figures that are
  visible and available, with no thought of what
  information may be needed but unknown or hidden;

- Excessive medical costs;

- Excessive legal liability costs, swelled by lawyers who work on contingency fees.[24]

Except, perhaps, for the last two items on the above list, all these "sins" of management refer to beliefs, policies, and practices so firmly entrenched that many, maybe most, American managers see them as basic truths.

For example, in American organizations managers typically assume that every employee has his or her own goals and that each department or division has its own aims. A common view is that it is only natural that these various parties compete to get what each wants. They presume that this will be best for the organization. But this is rarely the actual outcome. Much more often competition over multiple goals within the organization leads to conflicts and hard feelings. Compromises that result usually neither satisfy the parties nor benefit the organization. These conditions are what Deming refers to when he speaks of a "lack of constancy of purpose."

Most American firms also accept the "need" to satisfy stockholders with high dividends every quarter. The resulting focus on short–term profits, on quarterly stock dividends, and on driving up the value of the company's stock is so pervasive that two Harvard Business School professors pointed to this deadly disease as responsible in large part for what they called "managing our way to economic decline."[25]

The common acceptance of individual performance evaluations puts an inappropriate and dysfunctional emphasis on competition and looking out for one's own interests, above those of the organization as a whole. It also encourages the wrong use of data, that is, to judge results and control people (thus hoping to improve the results). The effective use of data involves understanding and improving the operations that produce those results.

In a *Wall Street Journal* interview, Deming said, "We rank people with incentive pay, annual appraisals . . . [but] judging people is not helpful . . . Ever heard of a bank that closed? Do you think it closed because of sluggishness and errors, mistakes at the tellers' windows, mistakes in bank statements, mistakes in calculation of interest? Don't be silly. It closed because management made bad loans. That's from incentive pay and ranking people. A bank lending officer has a quota to lend $83 million per month. He does it, and can you blame him? That was his job. Other lending officers do the same. And the bank gets into trouble."[26]

Americans are so mobile that we sometimes forget that it was not always this way. Deming observed that Americans put entirely too much emphasis on the "lifetime" job guarantee that some (and by no means all) Japanese companies give their workers. He points out that we do not emphasize enough that most Japanese companies give this sort of guarantee to their *managers*. This removes the need for job–hopping and increases the chances that managers will be committed to the organization and its purpose.

Finally, Deming notes that American managers often have at their fingertips massive compilations of data. Just as often, however, these data are useless for controlling or improving quality. That is, we try to use the information we happen to have or know how to get, without even asking why or for what purpose we need that information. "Costly computers turning out volumes of records is not quality control," says Deming.[27] Only by asking the right questions can one figure out what sort of data, what numbers, what figures are necessary.[28]

It may seem that we have been uncritically favorable toward Deming and his ideas while downplaying or ignoring the importance of others such as Joseph M. Juran, Kaoru Ishikawa, and Armand Feigenbaum.[29] After all, many people, both Japanese and Americans, have made important contributions to the development of TQM.

Moreover, for all his contributions, Deming is also known as a classic curmudgeon, so set in his views that he cannot conceive of other possibilities. And he is a colorful speaker, often embarrassing his hosts with comments not just blunt but profane!

We focus so much on Deming not because he is the best known or the most colorful of the "quality gurus" (though he is both). Our reason is simple. Deming's approach comes closer than any other to recognizing that only when top management makes a real commitment to creating a TQM culture is there the slightest hope that TQM will be attained.

Deming's approach is really an approach to management, a prescription for building the sort of culture that will support TQM. By defining positive aims as well as identifying the negative barriers that must be overcome, Deming's approach offers management a comprehensive system for achieving TQM. His system starts with but goes far beyond statistical process control and the other tools and techniques that have come to be incorrectly identified as TQM. It is Deming's new philosophy of management that is at the heart of TQM. Before exploring that philosophy in detail, however, we will first look at how it works — through tools — and then at how it involves the customer.

Chapter Two

TQM Tools and Techniques

In a way it is easier to explain how TQM works than it is to define what it is. That is, TQM works because of the organization's culture, through the organization's structure and management processes, and by means of various tools and techniques that employees learn to use. It may sound too simple but it's still true that TQM is based mostly on rational thinking and problem solving. However, to enable people to think and act rationally, organizations require complex and unusual cultures.

Deming has observed that in America plant managers often start the day with reams of computer–generated statistics. While these data may spell out in detail all the plant's quality problems, they usually tell the manager nothing at all about how to correct those problems. Simple rational thinking could, however, lead to a short report that, in Deming's words, "would tell [the manager] that at ten o'clock yesterday morning something went wrong on the line. At the same time, a new supplier's material went into use; the reason for the problem is a characteristic of the new material . . .. Too many companies," Deming concludes, "try to get along by using hardware instead of brains."[30]

The use of tools and techniques is the most visible evidence of TQM. It is, however, also the most superficial indicator of TQM and cannot be relied on as such. Statistical tools alone cannot lead to quality or TQM. The respected American quality consultant

Joseph M. Juran has said that "a good way to lose time in improving quality is to focus on tools and try to apply them."[31]

Juran's approach to quality, like Deming's involves the use of a number of tools. But, again like Deming, Juran recognizes that while they are necessary and useful, tools alone cannot lead to TQM. The most basic and general tool is brain–power and rational thinking. This is, perhaps, expressed most clearly in terms of the Plan–Do–Check–Act (PDCA) cycle, a technique made popular by Deming (but attributed by him to his mentor, Walter Shewhart; Deming always calls it "the Shewhart cycle").

The four steps in the cycle involve exactly what they state. First, *plan* carefully what is to be done. Next *do* it, that is, carry out the plan. Third, *check* to see what the results were, whether the plan worked as intended or whether the outcomes were different, perhaps even undesirable. Finally, *act* on the results, both positive and negative. This means identifying what worked as planned and what did not, then taking these results into account to develop an improved plan and start a new PDCA cycle. The four–step PDCA sequence is really nothing more than a straightforward rational problem solving process.[32]

The Seven Old Tools

Rational problem solving is what Deming had in mind when he said that organizations need more brains, not more machines. Admiral Grace Hopper, who helped design the first computer and develop the first computer language, observed that organized data, the raw "facts," forms information. But information, Admiral Hopper went on to say, is not worth much until the human brain processes it and turns that information into *intelligence.*

Computers and MIS (management information systems) do a wonderful job of turning data into information, producing massive automated reports on demand. However, only the human mind can make sense of what is happening to cause problems. To do this people do not usually need huge stacks of computer print-outs. What they do need is carefully-designed, timely, and accurately-tallied counts, presented in straightforward ways. Even more important is thinking through what one *wants* to happen and figuring out how to *make* it happen. In this sense, problems arise when something doesn't work as we planned or expected.

The jargon of quality control, SPC, and TQM includes the "seven old tools." The term "old" is used to set them apart from various "new" statistical tools. These new tools are much more sophisticated and complex, but they are not really required for TQM. In fact, the seven old tools are far more important, because *all* tools are really just procedures for counting, that is, for collecting and presenting data. There are only two requirements. First, the data must show clearly when things are not working as planned or expected. Second, the presentation should make it as easy as possible to identify the underlying causes of problems. The seven old tools are useful for identifying both common and special causes of work process problems.

We have provided brief descriptions and illustrations of the seven old tools in Appendix A, rather than in this chapter. We did this for a reason. Our purpose here is not to focus on these tools but to point out that all too often tools and techniques become the focus of all TQM-related activities. When this happens, as we illustrated in Chapter One, the TQM effort is almost sure to fail. But our point is not that the tools are unimportant, only that they can act as blinders and prevent people from seeing and dealing with the far more important elements of TQM, customers and culture.

Our descriptions of the seven old tools, in Appendix A, are very brief, even sketchy. Study and practice are needed to master each of these tools. That is precisely what Deming insists on when he advises that management must provide on–the–job training along with "a vigorous program of education and self–improvement" for all employees.[33]

Most of the seven old tools have been used for many years, some as long ago as the mid–1800s. Like the quality circle technique, it is not the tools themselves that are really new. Rather, it is their *use* as an integral part of TQM. The tools are just ways to display information visually, ways that help those responsible for quality and performance see how a system or process is operating. People can then interpret the information to identify problems. They can look for causes and proceed with a rational approach for solving whatever problems are identified.

New Tools

There are many other tools we could describe. Some are recommended by Deming, while others are not. Some (e.g., "Taguchi Methods") have become popular and are associated with one or another TQM "guru." There is also a set of "seven new tools," such as fault tree diagrams and factor analysis. These are statistical analysis techniques that are considerably more sophisticated than the seven old tools. The seven new tools are more likely to be used by engineers than by workers. Even so, many of these new tools can be and are being usefully applied to improve quality.[34]

Refinements of the tools and techniques described here, along with other, new, TQM methods, are common in Japanese organizations. For example, Matsushita Electric Works in Hakone uses a seven–

step technique called "Total Production Maintenance" (TPM).[35] First, the machine operators learn to clean their machines using standard cleaning procedures. (In this and many similar industrial operations each worker identifies closely and personally with the machine. Many machines have pictures of operators displayed on their sides, often with inscriptions like "I love this machine.")[36]

Once employees master the basic cleaning procedures they go on to learn to adjust the machine when something goes wrong. Third is a more complex and thorough grounding in cleaning and oiling. Next is responsibility for total inspection of the machine operation, using the manual. Fifth is total inspection followed by preventive maintenance. Sixth is understanding of product quality as it relates to the operation of every detail of the machine. At the seventh and highest level the operator alone becomes responsible for total preventive maintenance. It takes three years, on the average, for an operator to become qualified at the fifth level.

Another Japanese organization uses a different version of TPM called "the five s's" (sometimes also called "the four s's plus s"). This is because in Japanese the words "cleaning" (seiri), "tidiness" or "arrangement" (seiton), "sweeping/washing" (seiso), and "cleanliness" (seiketsu) all start with "s." The fifth "s" stands for the Japanese word for "discipline" (shitsuke). This is a more general concept compared to the other four s's, each of which represents a very concrete activity related to maintaining the physical plant area.

There are now available many books that describe one or another of the basic or advanced TQM tools and techniques, often in great detail. Japanese organizations constantly invent new TQM program elements like the two just described. Part of the TQM philosophy is that there must be continual improvement. To stick with current technology is to go backward. This applies both to tools and techniques for quality control and to the production or service technology of the organization.

Despite these continued advances, one must always keep in mind that the *tools* and *techniques* are not TQM. Not even training every employee how to use these tools and techniques will effectively implement TQM. TQM only operates when the value of quality for customers is an important part of the organization's culture.

The Tools Are Not TQM

People often confuse TQM with tools like those described here, with techniques such as quality control circles and using "nominal group" problem solving meetings, or with training activities that teach employees to use these tools and techniques. But tools, techniques, and training are just the most visible, superficial aspects of TQM. Tools are necessary but not sufficient for TQM. When made the focus of TQM, tools and techniques can even prevent the organization from taking the additional steps needed for TQM. In this way an overemphasis on tools, in the mistaken belief that the tools are TQM, can lead the organization in the opposite direction, away from an organizational commitment to quality.

In recent years many organizations excitedly adopted one or more of the tools and techniques described above, often at great cost. Typically they dropped them not long afterward (or maintain them only in a ritual, practically meaningless form). This happens when the underlying TQM value — the overriding importance of quality for the customer — is neither recognized nor part of the organization's culture.

This is what Deming discovered after World War II; despite his success at training workers and engineers throughout the U.S. to use his tools and techniques, his efforts, for the most part, came to nothing because management had not adopted the philosophy that the tools and techniques were intended to support. According to Halberstam, Deming continued for a time to train young engineers, but, as Deming later put it, "I was lighting a lot of fires, but they were all going out."[37]   His observations and discussions with managers and others helped Deming figure out why. He concluded that it was the lack of management interest and support that led organizations to abandon his earlier teachings and that dissipated the effects of his post-war efforts.

Fortunately, for the Japanese, Deming recognized this and, as detailed earlier, focused on gaining the commitment of Japanese top managers. And it would be wrong to fail to mention that, in recent years, some American executives and corporations have also made that commitment; while the number is small it should not be neglected.

But what exactly is this commitment? Is it to the abstract ideal of quality? We think not. Quality itself is what the commitment is about, but is not the whole of the issue. To fully understand TQM we must ask, "Quality for what?"   Before turning to the key elements of the new philosophy of TQM we must first answer this very basic question.

Chapter Three

Quality for the Customer

The various tools mentioned and described in the Chapter Two all aim to improve the quality of a product or service. This means studying and improving organizational processes, especially how products are made or services delivered. But it can be easy to forget that TQM is not a search for quality as some sort of "holy grail" or high tech ideal.

General Motors recently developed a new high technology "heads–up display," or HUD, that flashes dashboard data (fuel, speed, etc.) on the windshield. Drivers can see the information without taking their eyes off the road. However, despite a relatively low cost there have been few takers. Only about 6000 of almost 600,000 potential buyers actually ordered the device, for a sale rate of just over 1%. A GM official said, "We gave people whiz–bang technology that they did not want, did not value and weren't ready to use."[38]

The reason to be concerned with quality is that quality is the customer's concern. Juran addresses this issue when he says, "Quality is fitness for use."[39] Thus, Juran recognizes that it is the user who is really the concern, not some abstract ideal of quality. Deming, too, links quality to the customer when he states that by quality he means " . . . economic manufacture of product that meets the demands of the market."[40] According to Deming it is market demand, that is, the customer, that defines quality. Armand

Feigenbaum is even more direct when he observes, "Quality is what the customer says it is."[41]

This means that management must actively reach out to identify and understand the needs and desires of customers. The effort must be continual, since customers' needs and desires will change over time. The successful family–owned department store, Nordstrom's, maintains such an orientation. Nordstrom's is quite profitable and its salespeople earn among the highest wages in the industry, all despite relatively high prices. The key is commitment to the customer. Nordstrom's CEO recently said, "All of us in the generation now at the top started out as shoe salesmen, serving the customer by sitting at his or her feet and fitting shoes."[42]

The basic importance of a concern about quality for the customer is illustrated by comparing two very successful competitors, Stew Leonard's dairy store, in Norwalk, Connecticut, and Wegmans Food Markets in upstate New York.[43] In an article in *Nation's Business,* Michael Barrier shows that while the two organizations have very different market strategies they share an exceptionally strong concern over quality for the customer.[44]

Stew Leonard and Danny Wegman have visited each other's stores. Neither is overly impressed. Leonard ridicules Wegmans' 57 types of mustard on the shelves; Stew Leonard's carries just two. Danny Wegman retorts, "We're not subscribers to niche marketing. . . . Stew wants you to shop elsewhere, so you'll . . . appreciate what he's doing. We just want you to appreciate what we're doing. We don't want you to have to go anywhere else for anything you need . . . ."[45]

But neither niche marketing, like Leonard's, concentrating on superb quality and service with a limited line, nor "full service," providing every possible item variety customers might desire, is the answer. What both Stew Leonard's *and* Wegmans do is concentrate on what customers want and provide that at the highest level of quality. Tom Leonard searches for customer complaints, not compliments; he says, "I thank them so much for calling, because I can go out and solve the problem right now." Stew Leonard, Jr., runs a focus group discussion with a dozen randomly selected customers once a month, to get ideas for improvement.[46]

Wegmans not only makes sure that customers get the variety they want, it concentrates on being part of the communities it serves. Wegmans uses focus groups, too, but it also has a scholarship program for kids who bag groceries (there are over 17,000 employees, in all). And Wegmans made a conscious decision not to build "superstores," in order to stay close to customers at the local, store level.[47]

Both Leonard's and Wegmans invest extensively in employee job training, and both have profit sharing plans. Both promote from within (and not just family, though both are family–owned). All three of Wegmans vice presidents have spent their work lives in the company, starting as teenage baggers.[48] Although the two firms look very different and appear to have different operating strategies, a closer look shows that they are actually quite similar.

Some, actually quite a few, American organizations have gotten beyond a focus on the tools of TQM to focus on quality for the customer. It has become less rare to hear that an organization has the aim of quality and customer satisfaction above all else. One even finds evidence of such goals in organizational practices. And employees are often well aware of the need for quality for the customer. Despite such positive indicators, an evident concern for the customer and quality is not always a sign of effective TQM.

More often the reason behind all this is a simple business value: maintaining market share and profitability.

Most observers of the auto industry agree that Ford Motor Company has made great strides in quality in recent years. However, in 1987 a senior insider noted that the changes initiated at Ford were not simply the result of an interest in the work of Deming (who had been called in as a consultant). Deming would never have been invited in, said this insider, but for the fact that Ford had lost two billion dollars in one year.[49] It was only such a staggering loss that motivated top managers at Ford to consider that they might have a problem.

A concern for the bottom–line is not a bad reason to examine TQM. It is, however, an insufficient force for establishing and maintaining a TQM culture. Years of effort by American auto makers, including Ford, have resulted in clear improvements in quality, by any objective measure. Still, Ford — like General Motors and Chrysler — remains behind the Japanese auto industry in quality and customer satisfaction.[50] Perhaps it is not surprising that in 1990 Ford lost over $500 million (and has lost even more in 1991).

Concern for profit alone cannot sustain TQM over the long run. The *real* issue is concern for the customer through quality. Deming suggests that if quality for the customer is the bottom line, then other things will follow, including profit.

Just saying it, asserting a concern with quality for the customer, is not enough. To succeed TQM must be grounded in the organization's culture. Slogans and the superficial trappings of a TQM culture — "Service America;" "Quality is Job 1" — cannot create or support a TQM culture. They may even contribute to the failure of TQM efforts. In his tenth point Deming warns against signs and slogans. Elsewhere he says, "Exhortations and platitudes are not effective instruments of improvement . . .."[51] Popular slogans are usually created and repeated without any concern for how to attain the aims they exult. This is, says Deming, like goals without plans or destinations without maps — useless. Eventually, people become tired and give up.

What happens, though, when management does adopt a real concern of quality for the customer as a driving value? People throughout the organization use some, perhaps many, TQM tools and techniques. Moreover, employees receive training in how to apply the tools and techniques to their work.

A closer look proves even more interesting. One often finds that the application of TQM tools and techniques in these organizations is not limited to the manufacturing, production, or direct customer service areas. Instead, there is a coordinated and integrated effort to apply TQM. This effort centers on what have come to be called "quality checkpoints." There are five primary quality checkpoints; we will define each, briefly.

The Five Quality Checkpoints

Think of manufacturing or service delivery as the flow of a stream. Suppliers and vendors provide various materials (sometimes information rather than physical). These raw materials then move through production points and work processes that "transform" them into outputs, finished products (or services). These outputs then go "out the door," delivered to clients and customers. There are, then, five specific points at which quality can be checked.

First, and most important, quality can be identified in terms of how well (and whether) a product or service meets the needs and desires of customers, in actual use. This is the first quality checkpoint. Far more common, quality is checked by final inspection of the product or service, on completion. Final inspection prior to customer delivery or use, is the second quality checkpoint. The third checkpoint involves the actual production or service delivery process. Statistical process control and many of the other tools discussed in Chapter Two (and Appendix A) were designed to assess quality in the process of production or service delivery.

The quality of the raw materials that are transformed into a product or service can be examined and assessed when the materials are first delivered by suppliers and vendors. This is quality checkpoint four. Finally, one might actually go to the suppliers and examine how they produce those raw materials, to assess the quality control they exercise. This is quality checkpoint five. We will examine each checkpoint to discuss what is and should be done.

Quality Checkpoint 1. It might seem logical to refer to the very first step in the manufacturing or service planning process, obtaining materials from suppliers, as the first quality checkpoint (QC1). Instead we look to the customer first. Deming and others point out that customers are even more important than the production process itself. Only when one knows what that customer needs, wants, and expects can one design production ("transformation") processes that will meet those desires. Then, of course, the organization must ensure that the production process is "in control," but that comes *after,* not *before,* finding out what customers want. Because TQM begins with the customer that is where we locate QC1. Obtaining accurate and timely information about the needs, wants, and expectations of customers is the top priority and the driving force of any TQM system.

Activities at QC1 include customer surveys, focus group sessions with clients, and open-ended customer interviews. (Recall that both Stew Leonard's and Wegmans use focus group sessions to get customers' ideas and better understand their needs.) When feasible and appropriate, many organizations include customers in product planning, engineering, and problem solving meetings. At QC1 an organization serious about TQM will use a variety of methods to learn what customers need, want, and expect.[52]

Quality Checkpoint 2. This is the point at which products leave the organization or, for services, the point of final planning and delivery (prior to customer use). This has, historically, been the primary focus of so-called quality control activities: check to see that the car runs properly, that all systems function as they should, before shipping it for sale; check to see that the rugs are now as clean as standards require; conduct a test to show that the copying machine now produces perfect duplicates.

Managements' narrow emphasis on this checkpoint led Deming to assert (as one of his fourteen points), "Cease dependence on mass inspection to achieve quality!" Even though it is far less important than some other checkpoints, many organizations still expend disproportionate resources and attention on QC2, and many so-called quality control departments are merely inspection units.

This is not to suggest that final inspection is unnecessary. It will always be important to make sure that defective products are not, through some accident, sent out to customers. Final inspection information may even, when channelled properly, be useful for quality improvement. But, when TQM is actually practiced and is part of an organization's culture, that organization really does cease to *depend* on final inspection to ensure quality. Quality is designed and built into a product or service, not correctively added on later.

Moreover, final inspection is accomplished using statistical sampling techniques, not by inspecting every item.

Quality Checkpoint 3. QC3 is located at the site of the production or work activity process itself. This is the focus of many of the tools and techniques developed for quality control. Statistical process control (SPC) is one of the most common tools used at QC3 (though it is not always applied appropriately). Shewhart, Deming, and others developed SPC for use in manufacturing but it and other statistical tools are now used in service organizations, too. (Actually, it was in the 1940s that Deming showed how SPC could be applied to clerical work.)

An emphasis on QC3 is certainly desirable, but many organizations, in their rush to apply TQM, overdo this emphasis. They fall into the trap of trying to improve *all* the many elements that make up the production process. Instead, they should concentrate on the few *critical* elements that are of the greatest importance for meeting defined quality requirements.

Recall that one of the seven old tools is the Pareto Chart. The classical economist Vilfredo Pareto first observed what has come to be known as the "Pareto Principle." This principle states that around eighty percent of all positive results are produced by just twenty percent of the efforts. Similarly, roughly eighty percent of all problems can be traced to approximately twenty percent of all possible causes. It is, then, the critical twenty percent that one must try to control. Trying to control everything means wasting most of one's time and effort working on the eighty percent of causes that account for only one-fifth of the problems.

Quality Checkpoint 4. This checkpoint concerns incoming quality assurance. The organization must make sure that vendors and suppliers provide materials, products, services, and information of the quality needed. Only then can the organization construct products and deliver services of the quality desired by its customers. QC4 is, along with QC2, one of the two checkpoints traditionally emphasized by American organizations. Deming's criticism of inspection as the primary method used to achieve quality applies to QC4 just as it does to QC2. That is, inspection at the door is necessary. However, it is often too late. The fifth and final quality checkpoint is more important.

Quality Checkpoint 5. Activities at QC5 aim to ensure that input materials, parts, and supplies are designed and produced to specifications. This means working with suppliers and vendors to give them the information they need to deliver materials of the quality the organization requires. It is not uncommon for an organization committed to TQM to work with its suppliers to design the parts and materials they will deliver to the organization. In fact, engineers and technicians may even assist the supplier in identifying problems using TQM tools. More TQM organizations are, like Motorola, insisting that suppliers adopt a TQM approach.

Deming adamantly emphasizes the importance of QC5. One of his fourteen points exhorts organizations to "end the practice of awarding business on price tag alone." Instead of basing such decisions on price, Deming advises organizations to find quality-conscious vendors who are responsive to their customers' needs. Organizations should select on the basis of their record of quality and their commitment to learn and apply TQM. Then, suppliers are treated as part of the organization's team.

In Chapter One we commented on Wal–Mart's strategic change, from going "to the mat" with suppliers to negotiate the best possible deal to developing long–term cooperative relationships based on concern for quality. The strategy has paid off, resolving concerns about continuing expansion — as demonstrated when, in 1990, Wal–Mart surpassed Sears as the nation's largest retailer.

Procter & Gamble was one of the suppliers that Wal–Mart first went to, in 1988, to establish a "partnership" arrangement. P&G found this worked so well that it began a program to develop similar partnerships with other retailer–customers, like K mart. Both firms have created teams, including sales, purchasing, and data processing experts, to work together as partners. P&G now has more than 120 such teams working with different customers. In some cases cash register data goes directly to P&G to track inventory and automatically replenish stock.[53] A wide variety of other large suppliers are active in partnership arrangements. This includes Kraft General Foods, General Mills, Nabisco, and Johnson & Johnson. Kraft alone has almost 400 partnership teams.[54]

P&G has found it equally profitable to build partnerships with *its* suppliers. The firms has, for example, chosen to develop long–term partnership relationships with 15 major trucking firms, instead of bidding for the lowest price, its former practice. P&G estimates that overall partnerships with suppliers and customers has saved the company about $500 million per year, and figures it can double that.[55]

The various activities that occur at QC5 are driven by the needs and desires of customers. This is why organizations that are most advanced in applying TQM emphasize the connection between QC1 and QC5. They use QC1 information to define for suppliers and vendors the precise characteristics they require of the materials they obtain from their QC5 "partners."

The Quality Management Process

Organizations with a strong focus on quality for the customer recognize and attend to the five quality checkpoints. They also realize that the checkpoints are related to one another in a *circular* rather than in a *linear* fashion. They see QC1 as the most important quality checkpoint, but they also recognize that under-standing the connection between QC1 and QC5 is essential.

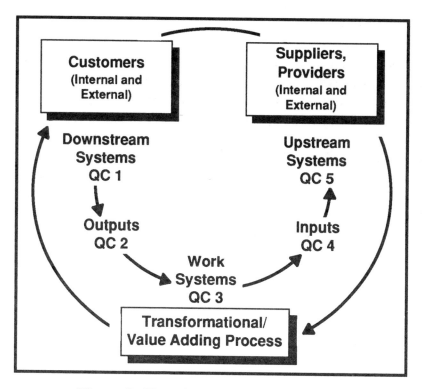

Figure 2: The Five Quality Checkpoints

The cycle shown in Figure 2 is the quality management process.[56] This process is at the heart of how TQM actually operates. An organization must recognize and manage all five quality check points. This means linking customers' needs, wants, and expectations — defined at QC1 — to every part of the process, all the way to the suppliers of raw materials. This is a difficult and sophisticated task. It is relatively easy to see how the customers' desires define quality as it comes "out the door" at QC2. It is harder to see how what customers want can (and must) connect with product design and with control over the manufacturing process (QC3). It is most difficult to carry this all the way to the raw materials at QC4 and suppliers at QC5.

We have tried to illustrate this in Figure 2 by showing arrows going clockwise, from supplier to work process to customer. At the same time, the "flow" of quality checkpoints is shown starting with the customer (QC1) and going on to work process output (QC2), to the work process itself (QC3), to work process inputs (QC4), to suppliers (QC5), in a counter–clockwise sequence. This makes for difficulty in the quality management process, analogous to the difficulty faced by salmon trying to swim upstream against the force of the river's current. And still another level of difficulty is in coordinating and managing the two processes, the actual work flows from suppliers through work systems to customers and the quality management process that goes in the reverse direction. The two are obviously closely related, yet they flow in opposite directions.

Many Japanese organizations both recognize and act on the concepts illustrated in Figure 2. One way is through "quality function deployment," a sophisticated technique designed to translate the importance of quality for the customer (defined at QC1) back to each prior process and checkpoint.[57] Teams, groups, and departments treat those at "downstream" organizational sites as their customers (with requirements based on what external,

QC1, customers desire). For a production group the immediate internal customer might be the shipping unit that deals with their output. The quality requirements of the shipping group will depend on product characteristics important for the shipping unit to do its work properly while ensuring that the product they ship meets the needs of *their* customer, the sales unit.

Another way to improve the quality management process is through a technique called "design for manufacture." This approach fosters new and more effective collaborative work relationships between engineering and production units. Using the traditional approach an engineering unit designs a new product and then ships off the plans to the production division. But often the production unit encounters problems that engineering design never considered. Solving those problems results in delays and added development costs. Using the "design for manufacture" technique the two units, engineering and production, form teams that work together from the start. They jointly develop a design intended to make production as easy as possible.

Bell Labs tried this approach in designing a new circuit board. Normally, design work takes place in New Jersey. Plans are then sent to the assembly plant in Oklahoma where production begins and problems are resolved as they are encountered. This time a team composed of engineers from both the New Jersey design unit and the Oklahoma plant worked together from the start. They worked out every detail in advance. They also anticipated many production problems that would have otherwise turned up later and would have cost much more to correct than to avoid. But even more, the overall quality of the product was improved. Compared to a prior, similar project that had been conducted the old way, the final testing unit found 60% fewer software errors.[58]

Of course, for every unit, upstream and downstream, the most basic and crucial product quality characteristics depend on what the final customer desires (defined, again, at QC1). TQM succeeds only by incorporating a concern about quality for the customer throughout the organization. Some organizations focus on one or another aspect of TQM — quality improvement, key process improvement, satisfaction surveys, and the use of various statistical tools, for example. But TQM depends on integrating these and other quality concerns, on dealing with them as part of a coherent and consistent management approach. Only organizations that manage each of the five quality checkpoints effectively, as part of a complete, continuous, and constant process, will successfully attain TQM. It is an overriding concern of quality for the customer that drives this process. Tools, techniques, and training are not enough.

Juran's TQM approach centers on how to organize and implement the TQM process so that the concern of quality for the customer pervades the organization.[59] He identifies three broad, basic approaches for doing this: quality planning, quality control, and quality management. Juran shows, in very specific and concrete ways, how to use these three approaches to construct a TQM system that is driven by a commitment to quality for the customer.

An integrated and systemic approach to the quality management process is necessary for TQM to take hold in an organization. Even this, however, is not in itself adequate to sustain TQM over the long run. There is still more to the development and operation of a TQM organization. For the long-term operation of an effective quality management process, as described in this chapter, an organization must have a *culture* based on, defining, and supporting TQM. This is what Deming calls a "new philosophy of management." In the next chapter we will examine the nature of this TQM culture, this new philosophy.

Chapter Four

The Cultural Basis of TQM

The hardest part of TQM to understand and to apply is the most important part: creating, nurturing and sustaining a culture based on TQM. But what is culture? What are its elements? And how do those elements relate to TQM? These are questions that go to the heart of the TQM approach. In this chapter we examine the nature of organizational culture and, specifically, TQM culture.

The Nature of Culture

Most social scientists who study organizations would agree that culture derives from — perhaps consists of — certain basic beliefs and values. These beliefs and values are defined and expressed by leaders and shared by the members of the organization.

Beliefs involve "if . . . then" statements. That is, "*If* I do this, *then* that will be the result." For example, a worker may know that statistical quality control data goes to the supervisor and then on to the department head. The worker may believe that when it is time for performance appraisals (and rewards) there won't be a raise if the "numbers" are "bad." The belief is, "If I give them accurate numbers, then they will use those numbers against me." Of course, such a belief (correct or not, and it is more likely than not to be correct) will stifle efforts to apply TQM tools; only "good" numbers will be reported.

One reason for such self–defeating beliefs can be found in the values they reflect. In the example given, the underlying value is "People should be controlled by rewarding or punishing them for their performance." This is very different from the value, "Processes should be controlled to result in excellent performance, to produce goods and deliver services of the highest possible quality." The first value really has little to do with organizational performance; the second relates directly to effective adaptation and achieving organizational goals.

The most important values and beliefs deal with three crucial areas of organizational functioning. These are *adapting* to change, *achieving goals,* and *coordinating* the work efforts of employees. The culture in TQM organizations — that is, the set of shared values and beliefs — makes sure that *adaptive change* is aimed at fulfilling customers' desires. One reason Ford lost its initial market advantage to General Motors, in the 1920s, was Henry Ford's refusal to develop new models that could compete with those introduced by GM.

TQM values define *goal achievement* as meeting customers' needs and desires. Another classic story has Henry Ford responding to a potential customer's query about color availability by saying, "You can have any color you want — as long as it's black."

The values and beliefs that make up a TQM culture make certain that organization members *cooperate* to carry out their work with a common aim: quality for the customer. In contrast, in *The Reckoning* Halberstam describes the vicious politicking and backstabbing that was common at Ford.

Consider the two contrasting values stated above. The value "People should be controlled by rewarding or punishing them for their performance" is inconsistent with TQM assumptions. It is also unrelated to the three crucial functions just defined, at least not in a positive way. In contrast, the second value, "Processes should be controlled to produce goods and to deliver services of the highest possible quality," supports the functions of adapting, achieving goals, and working together to satisfy the customer.

If TQM is to develop as an integral element of an organization's culture, a certain set of values and beliefs must be embedded and operate within that culture. Values and beliefs, remember, tell us what is "right" and what is "wrong," as well as the way things should happen ("if . . . then"). These values and beliefs must be based on TQM assumptions if they are to support TQM. We will specify and examine in some detail eight of the most important of these values and beliefs. Each represents an element of the organization's culture, as defined in the chart that follows.

Element I	Quality information must be used for improvement, not to judge or control prople.
Element II	Authority must be equal to responsibility.
Element III	There must be rewards for results.
Element IV	Cooperation, not competition, must be the basis for working together.
Element V	Employees must have secure jobs.
Element VI	There must be a climate of fairness.
Element VII	Compensation should be equitable.
Element VIII	Employees should have an ownership stake.

Eight Crucial Elements of Culture

Each culture element we will describe involves a single, clear value or belief. We will state that value as simply as possible, then discuss what it means and how it looks in action.

Element I: *Performance and quality information must go to those who use it to understand problems, develop solutions, and take action; such information must not be used to judge individuals' performance.*

We gave an example, above, of the possible consequences of providing higher level managers with accurate performance and quality information. This illustrated a major obstacle to TQM. That is, most American organizations use performance and quality information not to improve performance and quality, but in an attempt to control employees. This is done by monitoring and evaluating employees to make sure they "do it right" or, at least, do what management wants them to. With this aim in mind, management uses rewards for "good" results and punishments for "bad" results.

This goes directly against Deming's key principle, "Drive out fear." Organizations that operate this way, trying to control employees' performance by reward and punishment, make it certain that employees will not share with management accurate performance and quality information. After all, who would give higher–level management information that would result in negative outcomes for the person providing the data?

Whenever quality information goes "up the hierarchy" to a person's boss (or even higher), with the data tied to that person as a "cause," you can tell that the purpose of the performance and quality measurement system is to control individual employees, through rewards and sanctions. Such systems aim to control people, not to improve performance and quality. In these circumstances TQM has very little chance of succeeding.

One term for this type of measurement is "results metric." That is, the metric or measure assesses final results or outcomes. The idea is similar to the old "inspection" approach to quality control. That approach, we now know, is limited in the sort of corrections and improvements to work processes that can be made. Moreover, it cannot lead to *continuous improvement* in processes, to result in high quality products and services. But the benign use of results metrics is not what we speak of here. Using results metrics to judge employees' performance can lead to no benefit of any kind relevant for TQM.

New technology now allows supervisors to monitor employees' activities to a degree unknown and unimagined just a few years ago. There has even been discussion among scholars as to whether management would or should "recentralize" decision-making and control, by making use of such data collection approaches. Most of us are, for example, familiar with the approach used in many telephone companies to monitor the length of time operators spend with customers. Their purpose is to reduce the length of each call, thus increasing efficiency. Here is a case of results metrics fed directly to the supervisor. Supervisors tell operators to reduce the amount of time spent on each call. But the measure tells nothing about the causes of calls that last longer than the maximum permissible time.

Bell Canada was one of the companies that instituted monitoring for what was thought to be quality control. It wasn't working well;

employees — and the union — complained. In response the company designed an experiment, involving 2400 operators in Ontario. Operators were monitored as a group; individual times were no longer recorded, just the group's distribution and average. In the past when an operator's average time went above the desired standard of 23 seconds the employee would be disciplined. Now, when the group average went up managers would meet with employees to review the data, explore the problem, and develop a solution. Productivity went up and stayed up. The vast majority of employees thought that they were delivering better service, and the numbers backed them up. The experiment was extended throughout Bell Canada.[60]

In most Japanese organizations process performance data goes only as far as the person whose job it is to use that information to maintain and improve performance and quality. Data reported "up the line" on quality problems and actions taken to resolve them may be aggregated and examined by higher levels of management, but such information is not normally traceable to one or another worker or team. "Process metrics" is a term used to describe this approach to the use of performance and quality data by those who can apply it directly to identify problems, solve them, and make improvements. That is, the measurements center on the process of work, not just on the outcomes.

Management does sometimes need quality control information concerning what Deming calls "common causes" of quality problems. Common causes are part of the production process that management designed and set up. They are not the result of undesired variation introduced by the worker or by some other factors, which Deming refers to as "special causes." Workers must have the authority, as well as the responsibility, to use measure-ment tools to identify and eliminate special causes. But management must go farther and "empower" workers with the authority to identify and act on their own initiative to correct common causes of variation — the source of most quality problems.

Measurement systems designed to support TQM must be focused on improvement of processes, not on control of those responsible for work processes. This means emphasizing process metrics, not results metrics. The aim is to assess and improve work processes by identifying and correcting factors that cause undesired variation. This is very different from the notion of controlling *people*. The way in which measurement systems are designed and used will determine whether employees will support or subvert a TQM effort. Measurement system design and use is a crucial determinant of whether an organization's TQM approach will succeed or fail.

As in Bell Canada, Federal Express managers were concerned about the time telephone customer service agents were spending on each call. And, like Bell Canada, FedEx began a program of monitoring. Half of an agent's performance appraisal rating was based on doing better than the "standard" time of 140 seconds per call. But employees, and their managers, began to complain. Performance wasn't getting better, it was getting worse; agents had to be curt and abrupt with customers to "make the numbers." Top management listened and abandoned the fruitless employee–control–oriented results metrics program. Instead, a supervisor listens at random to each agent just twice a year. Soon afterward they meet to discuss what the supervisor heard. The emphasis is on customer service quality; time is not mentioned. Since starting to use this new approach not only has service improved, the average call length decreased.[61]

In systems that emphasize measurement for product or service improvement, using process metrics, the persons responsible for doing the job are the ones who collect and use quality information. No one else needs the data, at least not in a form that is traceable to an individual. This is because workers themselves take actions to solve problems identified using the performance and quality information collected.

Organizations with measurement systems that focus on monitoring people's performance, relying on the use of results metrics, present a dramatic contrast. A state of management by fear often exists: if your numbers aren't good enough you'll be punished. In such systems the point of gathering performance and quality data is not to identify problems and solve them. Instead, management's concern is controlling workers, usually by punishing those thought responsible for quality problems.

Trying to control employees instead of understanding and improving processes is stupid, as well as self-defeating. Deming points out that most quality problems are attributable to work processes, not to workers.[62] The work processes were created by management and are management's responsibility. Controlling people cannot improve quality. No matter what employees do they cannot change or correct the management-developed work processes and systems that they must use. Trying to control people also conveys and reinforces the wrong value: getting the right numbers, no matter what. This does not improve performance and quality.

Not only does the attempt to control people reinforce the wrong values and beliefs, it also results in a deadly by-product: fear. Deming refers to fear as the great enemy of quality improvement in any organization.[63] If one is afraid that poor performance or quality numbers will result in sanctions — a low pay raise, no pay raise at all, a reprimand or reduction in pay, or even the loss of one's job, for example — then no one is likely to provide management with "bad numbers." In such situations workers quickly learn that the only important job is producing "good" numbers. Making high quality products or delivering high quality services becomes irrelevant. In this way high quality and excellent performance, the essential elements of goal achievement, become almost irrelevant; only *looking* good becomes important.

Element II: Authority must be equal to responsibility.

Those responsible for hands–on production or service activities must also have the authority to take positive actions based on performance and quality information. What this really means is making process control, production and service assessment and improvement, a basic part of employees' jobs. People must have the authority to control and improve the work for which they are responsible.

This culture element is based on the value that employees should control their own work activities, rather than following orders from above or performing a set of mindless, rote actions. In the language of modern human resource management, the term most often heard is "empowerment." That is, employees should be empowered to take the sort of actions that will lead to high quality and excellent performance. They should not have to obtain approval from above for every minor change that might be made in some set of "standard" procedures.

American organizations, both large and small, have discovered that empowering employees can have striking, positive effects. A worker at an IBM plant in Rochester, Minnesota spotted a defect on a computer storage device and shut down the line. This saved IBM the cost of correcting defects, as well as the potentially greater cost of lost customer satisfaction. This IBM facility won the U.S. Department of Commerce 1990 Malcolm Baldrige National Quality Award.[64]

At a smaller operation, Johnsonville Foods in Sheboygan Wisconsin, empowered workers buy equipment, write budgets, train one another, cut their hours when necessary, and even hire and fire one another.[65] The owner, Ralph Strayer, says "It isn't a soft or crazy deal. I'm a real hard–nosed pragmatic guy. . . . Teach people to do for themselves; this way you get a far better performance." The figures back him up: since he empowered employees sales have increased by over 20% per year while productivity has increased 50% in the past four years.

Federal Express won a 1990 Baldrige Award, the first service company to compete successfully for the Award. Tom Peters tells a now–legendary story about a "junior telecommunications expert"

> who, following a blizzard in the California Sierras, was faced with the prospect of having no phone service for several days. . . . With . . . no need to seek approval from above he rented a helicopter (using his personal American Express card), was dropped onto a snow-bound mountaintop, trudged three–quarters of a mile in chest–deep snow, and fixed the line to get Fed Ex back in business.[66]

Peters goes on to note that while extraordinary, this behavior was no fluke accident, that "all workers are routinely expected to take whatever initiative is required to fix problems and/or extend first-rate service to a customer."[67] This sort of expectation has always been characteristic of Federal Express. But what of organizations in which such expectations have never before existed?

Even a company that has not traditionally given employees authority can change. Up until 1980 Johnsonville Foods was run like most other companies: Ralph Strayer, the owner and CEO, made all the decisions. Despite continued growth and profitability he was worried; employees didn't seem to care about their work. Mistakes and accidents were on the increase. Incorrect ingredients were added to a product; a forklift was driven through a wall.

Strayer wanted a company in which everyone took responsibility — for the job, the product, and the company. But an attitude survey demonstrated that the opposite was the case, just as he had observed. After much thought, Strayer concluded that they were justified. He had made all the decisions; everyone else was just a "hired hand." It took him two years to begin to change, by giving people the authority to deal with their responsibilities.

In one plant, he reports,[68] employees were unhappy about working weekends to make deadlines. Strayer asked plant managers to get the workers to figure out why weekend work was needed. They found that during the week machine downtime averaged between 30% and 40%. The most important causes were absenteeism, people late for their work shifts, and other factors attributable to the employees themselves. By addressing these causes, employees reduced downtime to 10%; weekend work became unnecessary.

It took Ralph Strayer several years more to fully involve employees in making work decisions, from tasting the sausage for quality to analyzing and solving production problems. But rejects went from five percent to below one-half of one percent.

The manager of an employee-run cereal plant points out that "Nobody knows the job as well as those doing it. If you empower those people to make the decisions they make good ones." She goes on to say, "It's not a social experiment. It makes good business sense." When employees are empowered to make decisions they often save the company substantial sums of money. At Chaparral Steel, in Texas, a lathe worker found a new machine that cost only half the $1.5 million that had been budgeted. Substantial quality improvements can occur when employees have the authority — are empowered — not just to identify problems but to make decisions and take actions to solve those problems on their own initiative.

To be effective empowerment requires what some call "enabling conditions." That is, empowered employees must understand the concepts behind TQM. They must learn to use measurement tools (such as SPC) to identify problems. And performance and quality information must be used for performance and quality improvement, not to try to control employees. When these conditions are met, workers will have the knowledge, the skills, and the opportunity to take corrective actions that solve problems.[69]

The only limit on empowering employees to solve problems should be that the problems are in the employees' own areas and don't directly involve others. When other employees or units are involved, they must also have a say in problem solving. This is important because many problems arise at organizational "interfaces," the points at which one work process must be coordinated with another. Recall that the TQM management process described in Chapter Three calls for each employee or team to consider the next person or group "downstream" as the "customer" for that person's or group's output. Ensuring quality for the customer means making sure that the customer's needs and desires are known and are the basis for action; this includes "internal customers" as well as the "final" external customer.

Element III: There must be rewards for results.

There must be recognition for achievement, both symbolic and in terms of material rewards. All too often rewards are just symbolic . . . a certificate, a pin, or the employee's name on a plaque or in a newsletter story. This sort of symbolic recognition is important, and we aren't suggesting that it be eliminated. However, symbolic rewards should be accompanied by material rewards such as cash bonuses or special privileges that employees see as important.[70]

Material rewards support and reinforce the value that it is good to achieve high quality and productivity, or that problem solving (effective adaptation) is good. If such achievements are good, one would wonder why management fails to reward them. If problem solving is important, one must ask why management's recognition of effective examples is limited to symbolic rewards. Eventually one realizes that such achievements, in quality, productivity, or problem solving, are simply *not* valued.

To best reinforce TQM values, rewards should operate at the organizational level, at the group level, and at the individual level. In the U.S. rewards are often directed only to the individual. Moreover, rewards are then often attached to the wrong values, values that run counter to those that support effective, adaptive problem solving and achievements in quality and productivity.

In Japan, a firm's good performance (as measured by productivity and profit) frequently yields a bonus to employees equivalent to a substantial portion of employees' yearly salary. Thus, recognition for achievement occurs on the organizational level. In the U.S., too, more organizations are trying out formal plans for sharing with employees the results of their improvement efforts and thus rewarding employees for results. One especially well-known type of system is the Scanlon Plan, but there are many other formal "gainsharing" approaches.[71]

Globe Metallurgical, in Alabama, applied Deming's approach to win the 1988 Baldrige Award. Globe also reported quality–related savings of $10.3 million per year. This permitted raises averaging 6% per year and profit–sharing[72] payments of about $4000 per year for each employee. Johnsonville Foods also has a profit sharing system, as well as extensive employee involvement. Tom Peters reports that market share (in the Milwaukee area) rose from 7% to 50% over a recent ten–year period.[73]

When Virginia Fibre (a paper manufacturer) began operations in 1975, its founder Bob Macauley knew that he wanted to create a different kind of organization. He wanted everyone to be treated with dignity and respect and to feel free to help one another, with no restrictions on the tasks that one or another employee might be permitted to do. He and VF president Charlie Chandler realized that to attain the level of employee involvement and commitment they wanted, the organization would have to allow everyone to share in its growth and performance. They created an organization based on what they call a "Principles Partnership." Included was a system for sharing with employees the increased profits that result from performance and productivity improvements.

Management estimated how many tons of paper the machinery could produce, per day, and set that as the base. Each month the average daily tonnage produced is calculated. For every ten ton increment over the base everyone in the company receives a one percent bonus. This past year the firm has had two successive months in which the bonus was over 20% of monthly wages, paid to every person from the chairman to the most recently hired permanent employee.[74]

In some cases reward and profit–sharing plans work at the group rather than the organizational level. This is true, for example, of the TQM program at Motorola. Rewards go to teams or groups of employees, based on team efforts and achievements, rather than going to everyone in the organization.

The "standard" approach to rewarding employees in the U.S. is in terms of individual achievement. Organizations practicing TQM use this approach too. However, they apply it in ways that are very different from the merit pay and performance appraisal approach common in American industry. For example, Johnson-ville Foods, which ties bonuses to company performance (sharing almost 30% of pre–tax profits), also provides for individual rewards. While the firm gives no automatic cost of living or seniority raises, employees can increase their salaries by assuming greater responsibility. In some other organizations pay may be based, in part, on employees' skills. That is, in order to receive a pay increase an employee documents and demonstrates that his or her value to the firm has increased as a result of learning certain new skills.

Even in Japan recognition rewards occur on the individual level. For example, in some firms workers receive a small payment for *any* improvement suggestion (and a larger payment for an excep-tionally good one).[75] This supports the value of solving problems and coming up with ideas that result in effective adaptation. Individual rewards work best when they avoid pitting employees one against the other for a fixed quantity of money.[76]

In contrast to the varied approaches to reward just identified, most American firms are subject to Deming's "deadly disease" of individual merit rating and annual performance appraisal. This type of reward system has several negative effects. First, it emphasizes individual competition. Thus, when one person receives a very positive rating it often means that others must receive a low rating to maintain a "normal distribution."

As it happens, the notion of a normal distribution of work performance is not only false, it helps guarantee that overall performance will be less than is possible. That is, the assumption that performance must conform to a normal distribution, a "bell–shaped curve," places an artificial limit on performance. It directs attention toward the comparison of "good" and "poor" individual performers, that is, persons above or below the average. But this is not the relevant issue; TQM is a key to unlocking productivity and quality gains by raising the absolute level of system performance, raising the "average" itself. To do this the Wallace Company appraises performance solely on a group instead of an individual basis while Virginia Fibre focuses on team, rather than individual, objectives and accomplishments.

The idea of a normal distribution of performance naturally leads to comparisons between and among employees. This, in turn, reinforces competition, according to Deming. "Instead of working for the company, people compete with each other," he says.[77] Thus, when organizations rely on individual appraisal and merit ratings to assign rewards, employees will often forgo opportunities for productive collaboration and cooperation. Instead, they may engage in actions that will make them "look better" as individuals. The individual result is a higher performance rating — and a greater pay increase or bonus. But for the organization the outcome may be poor quality products and lower profits.[78]

The individual merit rating approach to reward, as traditionally applied, encourages the use of quality information to judge individuals. In this way information that might be used productively, for quality control and improvement, is made worthless. Information that is to be used to evaluate an individual — for example, to demonstrate one's achievements in an appraisal interview — is certain to be as distorted as possible in the positive direction. How else would one have the appearance of effective performance? When such use of information is encouraged, the use of information for quality improvement is discouraged. No one wants to risk sharing information that might prove he or she "has problems."

We have, like Deming, argued against merit rating and performance appraisal, as traditionally used. Especially damaging is the use of quality information to judge individuals. It may seem that we are contradicting the culture element being described, the value of rewards for results. At the least, one might conclude that there should only be rewards for group (or team) performance and to all employees, based on organizational performance. However, this is not so. Individual performance can be assessed in a manner consistent with and supportive of TQM.

And individual rewards for individual performance are *not* necessarily inconsistent with the use of information for quality improvement. Individual rewards can be based on skill improvement, on the development of new skills, on quality improvement ideas and actions, or on a variety of other performance–relevant factors. The only limit is the imagination of managers and employees. Individual rewards should not, however, be based on the assessment of individual productivity or, in particular, on measures of quality of product or service that are tied to the individual. The key here is understanding that rewards must be designed to recognize individuals' contributions to organizational performance, not as tools to control employees' behavior.

In sum, there are two important aspects to this culture element. *First,* employees must share in the outcomes of their efforts. This means that there should be both material as well as symbolic for the results they have helped achieve. *Second,* rewards should be designed at all levels, that is, for individuals, for groups or teams, and for everyone (based on organizational performance and outcomes).

A multi-level reward system creates a problem: making sure that the different types and levels of reward do not conflict. If individuals receive substantial rewards for improvement suggestions that work, but groups are also encouraged to develop improvement ideas and are rewarded by a team bonus, then a situation exists in which the team's members are being played off against the team as a whole. This is unwise and unhealthy. As we have pointed out, it is possible to structure individual rewards that do not conflict with group rewards. An employee's basic pay rate might, for example, go up when new skills are learned. This does not conflict with team rewards based on team improvement efforts.

Rewards, both symbolic and material, are limited only by people's imagination and creativity. The key is consistency among individual, group, and organizational rewards. Achieving such consistency is often a challenge.

Element IV: *Cooperation, not competition, must be the basis for working together.*

All too often U.S. organizations reward employees for individual efforts but not for actions that contribute to team or organizational performance. Even worse, rewards often accrue to a person when that individual's actions are detrimental to group or organizational performance. Earlier we quoted Deming as pointing out how in Japanese organizations everyone acts as part of a team, for the good of the entire organization. In American organizations it is often a matter of every person for him– or herself.

One way to move away from competition and toward greater cooperation is to design jobs so that employees work in teams. Such change is happening all over the U.S., in almost every industry. This started in the late 1960s, as experiments in new plant design using "socio–technical systems." The work was set up to be done by teams, operating with a high degree of authority and autonomy — and with no formal supervisors. In the early days some of these experiments floundered but by the late 1970s there were hundreds of successes. By the late 1980s they numbered in the thousands.

Richard Walton, of the Harvard Business School, has been active in these experiments from the very start. He reports that over the past twenty years there has been a clear movement in American organizations, away from efforts to control workers and toward reliance on employees' commitment.[79] Walton sees this as closely connected to the increasing use of self–controlling work teams. Joseph Juran suggests that a major trend for the 1990s will be an even greater emphasis on these self–managing teams.[80]

A recent survey of Fortune 1000 firms substantiates Juran's prediction. The survey showed that 46% (of those responding) had some self–managing teams. In 1987 the figure was only 27%.[81] Johnsonville Foods uses the self–managing team approach along with employee empowerment. One team even designed its assembly line. Juran has observed that when workers design or redesign their own jobs it restores planning to where it once was — and belongs — that is, at the operational level. What is more,

Juran points out, planning by work teams is much more sophisticated than when management does all the planning.[82]

As a side–effect of team–based job design, employees gain
authority commensurate with increased responsibilities. Another
effect is to make it more difficult (as well as unnecessary) for
managers to try to use results metrics to reward or coerce employees to achieve better performance outcomes.

In Japan the cooperative team ethic is so strong that workers see
themselves as team members even when tasks are not designed to
be done by a group of people working together. In the United
States it will take more to create the sort of underlying value of
cooperation that seems to come so easily in Japan.[83]

Element V: Employees must have secure jobs.

Japanese firms are known for their reluctance to lay off employees,
even under the most adverse business conditions. A surprising
number of the very best American firms, companies such as
Hewlett–Packard and IBM, have long adopted the same practice of
no layoffs.[84] Such a policy is probably one of the most powerful
strategies for organizations wishing to "drive out fear."[85]

An individual with years of experience as corporate director of
training for a very large retailing conglomerate observed to us that
security goes beyond guarantees against layoffs. In many organizations, this person noted, the common adage is "Screw up the first
time and I'll get you; screw up the second time and you're history!"
Instead, what is needed is the commitment of managers at all levels
to do everything possible and reasonable to coach employees to
success. Too many American businesses treat employees like

inventory that can be replaced at will. But only when employees feel a sense of job security will they take risks to make improve- ments. At a time when many organizations are "downsizing" by eliminating jobs, employees' fear of making mistakes that might cost them their jobs can greatly reduce their potential effectiveness.

American management has often viewed performance and produc- tivity improvement as a matter of driving down costs. This, too, has negative effects on job security. Labor force reductions, with the same or more work done by fewer employees, are an obvious way to reduce costs. The belief that it will at times be necessary to eliminate jobs to reduce costs may be why so few American firms provide secure jobs. But these assumptions about reducing costs are false. Research and practice show that the best way to improve performance *and* reduce costs is to focus on quality improvement, with an emphasis on what customers desire. Peter Drucker has observed that work must be done right or not done. Trying to get something done cheaply, by using inferior materials and hoping it will be all right, is foolish.[86]

It is short-sighted to seek to cut costs by cutting corners. It is even more self-defeating to try to reduce costs by laying off employees. Doing so shows that the organization does not value people. In Chapter One we gave the example of a firm in which a quality circle program failed after half the work force was laid off. Some organizations start such programs as a cost reduction technique and not because of a commitment to quality. It is difficult to imagine why employees who see their coworkers laid off to reduce costs would want to help the organization make a better product or deliver a better service.

Paradoxically, trying to reduce costs by eliminating people may have just the opposite effect. People who feel that their jobs are at risk are not likely to spend their time looking for ways to save on costs.   In fact, they may create new (though unnecessary) activities, to make themselves look less dispensable, thus adding new costs.   Organizations that do not provide employees with secure jobs are unlikely to find success through TQM.

Element VI: Everyone must perceive a climate of fairness in the organization.

Recent research shows that by their actions managers create organizational "climates." These climates can be characterized as fair or as unfair, as seen by employees.   But fairness is a much more complex issue than many people assume. Some of the most respected philosophers, from ancient times (e.g., see Aristotle's *Nicomachean Ethics*) to the present (e.g., see John Rawls' *A Theory of Justice*), have struggled to define the nature of fairness. Part of the problem is that fairness is in the eye of the beholder. Two people can look at the same situation and one may judge it as grossly unfair while the other finds nothing amiss. The solution is simple in one way and complicated in another sense.

The simple part is that fairness depends mostly on managers' actual behaviors, especially the behaviors of top-level leaders. Managers can choose to act in ways that create a positive fairness climate. The complex part is that acting is far more difficult than deciding, involving interrelated behaviors that require skill and practice. Ten specific areas of action that help define the organizational climate of fairness are:

- actions that develop *trust*, such as sharing useful information and making good on commitments;

- acting *consistently,* so that employees are not surprised or taken aback by unexpected management actions or decisions;

- being scrupulously *truthful* and avoiding so-called "white lies" and actions designed to manipulate others by giving a certain (false) "impression;"

- demonstrating *integrity* by keeping confidences and observing basic ethical guidelines to show one's concern for others;

- meeting with one's employees to discuss and define exactly what is *expected* of them;

- making sure that people are treated *equitably,* that is, giving equivalent rewards for similar performance by different employees and avoiding actual or apparent "special treatment" for "favorites;"

- giving employees meaningful *influence* over decisions about their own work, especially how to accomplish their work goals and what to do about work problems;

- adhering to clear standards that are seen as *just* and reasonable, for example not giving praise out of proportion to accomplishments or imposing penalties disproportionate to an offense;

- demonstrating *respect* toward employees, showing by actions that one really cares about others and recognizes their strengths and contributions;

- following *"due process,"* that is, procedures that are open to public scrutiny and which permit everyone to participate actively in their application.

Many of these ten aspects of fairness relate to one or another of the other factors that support a TQM culture. Fairness is important for TQM because it is difficult if not impossible for employees to feel empowered, to believe that there will be rewards for results, or to act cooperatively unless they see conditions as fair.

One recent research study[87] showed that organizations with exceptionally positive climates of fairness are characterized by exceptionally low employee accident and sickness compensation costs. A climate of fairness acts against Deming's sixth and seventh deadly diseases — excessive medical costs and excessive legal liability costs, respectively. In sum, fairness is the foundation for many, and perhaps most, aspects of a TQM culture.

Element VII: Compensation should be equitable across organizational levels.

In Japan the CEO of a typical large corporation earns ten to twenty times as much as the lowest-level salaried employee; in 1990 the average for Japanese CEOs was 17 times the wage of an ordinary worker.[88] Thus, if an assistant bookkeeper makes about $18,000 the CEO of that corporation would probably earn the equivalent of about $306,000. (In Japan year-end bonuses equal to one-third or more of a person's annual wage are common in successful firms. Thus, the actual wages might be $25,000 and $425,000; the proportions are still the same.) This is close to what experts have suggested as the optimum ratio of pay for the CEO in relation to the lowest-paid employee. Peter Drucker, for example, has argued that CEOs should earn no more than about twenty times the pay of the lowest-level employee.[89]

In most large American firms, CEOs earn from 50 to 100 times as much as the lowest-level salaried employee (85 times was the actual average for 1990).[90] Not only is executive pay in the U.S. higher than anywhere else in the world, it is twice as high as in the two next-highest countries, Canada and Germany.[91] Such large pay differentials make fairness more difficult to achieve and may undermine some of the other TQM culture factors.[92] It may be unrealistic to expect compensation "compression" in American organizations similar to that common in Japan. Still, there is evidence that adjustments are being made that result in a smaller disparity between executives' and workers' pay.[93]

Whether or not the ratio of executive to worker pay changes, organizations can take actions that will reduce the negative effects of the disparity. For example, appropriate rewards for performance and employee ownership, both issues already discussed, can help make compensation practices more equitable. Eliminating special "perks" and status differences across organizational levels can also have positive effects; normally these factors emphasize pay differences. By means of these and other strategies some attention must be given to the issue of gross discrepancies in pay across organizational levels, if a TQM culture is to be established.

Element VIII: Employees should have an ownership stake in the organization.

In a recent best seller, CEO Harvey Mackay says, "Owning 1 percent of something is worth more than managing 100 percent of anything."[94] Research bears out Mackay's assertion. Employee-owned firms are, on the average, half again as profitable as comparable firms without some form of employee ownership.[95] In many American organizations management has discovered that employees' capitalistic economic stake in the firm seems to strengthen the other cultural factors we've been discussing. Total employee involvement becomes even more effective when workers have a stake in the firm as well as a say in work–related matters.

At Herman Miller, considered the maker of some of the best quality office furnishings in the world, all employees *must* own company stock. Eventually the firm will be completely employee–owned. In many other organizations employees become owners through one or another "ESOP" — employee stock ownership plan. Some of these plans operate as investment retirement funds, while others hold the stock in trust–like arrangements. Regardless of the technical structure of the plan, the common aim is to provide employees with an ownership stake.

While ownership can be a significant factor, it is not necessarily the most important factor. Of course, in some organizations, such as government agencies, publicly–owned agencies, or cooperatives employee ownership is not possible. The key is that employees must *feel* and *act* as though they are owners. Even when legal ownership of the organization is impossible, employees can have a sense of ownership over their work and actions. But this only happens when it is fostered by the culture created by top managers.

Understanding TQM Culture

We have discussed eight specific elements involved in TQM cultures. There are surely others, but we believe that the ones we have defined and discussed here are the most important. We have not tried to describe all cultural elements — that would probably be impossible. Our focus has been on the elements that create and maintain TQM, the ones that are crucial for TQM success.

The eight TQM culture elements are founded on certain values, the sense of what is right and what is wrong. They are based on specific beliefs about the way things work — and the way they should work — in the organization. We have tried to avoid philosophical discussions, in favor of practical specifics about the policies and practices that help define and shape culture. They do so by exhibiting, reflecting and, in concrete ways, supporting the values and beliefs that underlie TQM.

Some of the eight elements are relatively simple to implement, at least in concept. Setting up an employee stock ownership plan or a policy of job security, for example, is difficult only if management does not accept these concepts. Actually implementing an ESOP or a "no-layoffs" policy need not be an especially complicated undertaking.

Implementing other culture elements can be more complex and challenging. An example would be developing policies, systems, and practices that reward employees for results, and for team and organizational as well as individual performance. And it can be even more difficult to make some of the elements we have described a part of the organization's culture. Some obvious examples are developing a climate of fairness, instilling cooperation, and empowering employees.

In every case, however, the key is action. Leaders and managers construct and reinforce the organization's culture by their actions and practices. Culture is created by their daily decisions and behaviors. Culture is not a "mission statement" hanging on the wall. It is not a comment in a policy manual mentioning "employ-ee rights." It is not an isolated event in the company's history. It is not treating employees to a Christmas luncheon once a year. What, then *is* culture?

> *Culture is the cumulative perception of how the organi-zation treats people and how people expect to treat one another. It is based on consistent and persistent management action, as seen by employees, vendors, and customers.*[96]

Virginia Fibre Corporation has been working to create a TQM culture ever since it was founded more than fifteen years ago. Its president, Charlie Chandler, recently said of VFC employees and the culture they have created, "We have a special relationship where we can talk about anything within the company and the future of the company. . . . I can't imagine going back to where . . . there are sharks swimming down the hallway — each depart-ment trying to get one up on the other."

Only by actively implementing the eight TQM culture factors is the foundation of a TQM culture developed. The greatest difficulty is making a continuing, long-term commitment to TQM; Virginia Fibre has been at it for fifteen years. In the next chapter we will examine some of the ways this long-term commitment comes about.

Chapter Five

Creating and Leading a TQM Culture

Many of the culture elements defined in Chapter Four are implemented through organizational policies, plans, programs, and practices. In Chapter Two we discussed the statistical tools for applying TQM. Similarly, we think of these methods for constructing or changing organizational culture as "social" tools for developing TQM. Just as the seven old tools build quality through statistical process control, these social tools can build the culture to support long-term TQM. And like the statistical tools, some social tools are relatively simple and easy to apply while others are much more difficult to use, requiring considerable skill. We will look at some of these social tools, their use and their effects.

Even the simpler social tools call for a degree of skill and knowledge. The more complex social tools require leadership, visionary leadership. Top executives must act as leaders and become culture builders. These are the difficult issues we will explore by examining the nature of cultural leadership and, specifically, how visionary leaders build TQM cultures.

Social Tools to Develop Cultural Values

The social tools — management policies, plans, programs, and practices — establish and support the eight culture elements and the values that are at the heart of these elements. We will describe several of these social tools and examine, in particular, just how they relate to certain of the eight elements of a TQM culture.

Empowering through job design. Good job design[97] provides employees with greater control over their work. Control over decisions about how to do the job and how to solve work–related problems is especially important. This generally means that authority is commensurate with responsibility. "Empowerment" is the social science jargon term most often used to refer to this aim.

Some scholars suggest that empowerment necessarily involves a certain set of conditions, including elements of job design. First, workers must believe that their work efforts can result in positive outcomes. Workers must also feel competent and able to do their work effectively. This implies mastery of the knowledge, skills, and actions required to do one's job. The work itself must be designed to form a coherent "whole" job that has intrinsic meaningfulness. Finally, employees must have the authority to make work–related decisions on their own.[98]

One early report shows how both control and coherence can become a natural part of the job. This case involved the assembly of washing machine water pumps. The job was done on an assembly line basis by six operators, each of whom added certain parts to the pump chassis. This was changed so that a single person assembled an entire pump. Besides having a more complete job, workers could now control their own work pace. Employees were also responsible for inspecting and approving the finished pump. The result was shorter assembly time along with improved quality and reduced cost.[99]

Another job design study, in Great Britain, involved sales representatives.[100] The study was planned as a formal experiment.

One group of employees had their jobs changed in certain respects while another "control group" of sales reps continued doing the job the old way. Reps in the experimental group were, for example, given authority to determine the frequency with which customers would be visited. Previously, reps had to get their managers' approval of their sales visit schedules. Now, the reps were the only ones who kept and saw these records. This is consistent with our discussion of the first TQM culture element: information must be used for quality improvement, not to control employees. Sales reps were also given authority to settle customer complaints involving up to $250, on the spot. They could agree to accept return of faulty or surplus materials, even if the materials were old and obsolete. Reps also had authority to negotiate prices and to give discounts.

Fifteen sales representatives were in the experimental group, while another twenty-three served as the "control." Those in the control group did their jobs the old way. Neither group had an economic advantage, such as the biggest customers or the best-selling product line. Moreover, during the previous year the average performance for those in the two groups was about the same. The test was to compare sales during the experimental period with sales in the same period of the previous year.

After nine months, sales for those in the control group had declined about 5%, on the average. In contrast, sales reps in the experimental group increased their gross revenues by about 19% over the previous year. This represented an increase of over $300,000 in sales. In terms of performance the job design clearly payed off. How about employees' satisfaction with the changes? Reps in the control group were neither more nor less satisfied after the study than before. But those in the experimental group reported that they enjoyed their work more than in the past.

Good job design does even more than empower employees by giving them control over their own actions and a sense of achievement from completing a "whole" job. When properly carried out, job design also provides for team–based cooperative interactions with others.[101] The "classic" U.S. example of team–based work design is that of a pet food factory in Topeka, Kansas.[102] The plant was designed new from the ground up. Individuals were to have much greater authority than in traditionally–designed plants. They also had the skill to do many different parts of a job. The work was designed to be done by self–managing teams of seven to fourteen employees, with no first–line supervisors.

Teams not only worked as a unit, they solved problems as a group, distributed the work, made operating decisions, and even interviewed and hired new team members. Although the plant's performance was outstanding from the start, it took a relatively long time for the plant to become the model for the entire organization that top managers had planned. In part the plant was so effective that it made other, older plants "look bad." Managers were literally shunned by those in the other plants. In other words, when two organizational cultures collide, the one that survives may not be the one that is most effective and functional! Fortunately, top management remained committed to the new plant concept and, over the long haul, it became accepted and copied.

"Self–managing teams" have become very popular in the past few years.[103] The approach derives in part from the sort of "socio-technical system design" experiments just discussed. But its popularity does not come from companies' desires to copy interesting experiments. The increasing use of this sort of team work design is based on accumulated evidence that autonomous teams, with "whole" jobs and authority equal to responsibility, are a more effective and less costly way to get the job done.[104]

The three examples above, and hundreds of others, show that effective job design fulfills three basic adult human work needs:[105]

- the need for control over one's actions;[106]

- the need for achievement through accomplishment of complete tasks;[107] and,

- the need for work–relevant interaction with others.[108]

We believe that these three factors are the essence of participative management.   They are what make participative management work.[109] There are many approaches to job design but they are all variations on the same basic themes: increased control, more meaningful and complete activities, and team–based interaction.

It is probably something of an oversimplification to speak of job design as if it were a single, specific tool. Even so, as a general approach, job design is one of the best known and most widely used tools for building a TQM culture. Recall the eight culture elements we defined earlier. As described here, job design makes authority equal to responsibility (Element II). It instills cooperation and teamwork (Element IV). Job design supports a policy of rewards for results (Element III) and is consistent with the appropriate use of quality measurement (Element I). In sum, job design can have an important positive effect on several of the eight TQM culture factors; it is an important tool for building a TQM culture.

Encouraging employee ownership. In Chapter Four we mentioned several employee ownership programs (ESOPs, individual stock

purchase options, etc.). Of the eight cultural elements we identified, employee ownership, while useful and potentially powerful in
impact, is probably the least crucial for TQM. Some researchers,
and managers, used to think employee ownership motivates
employees and leads to positive effects from participative employee
involvement. More recent research, however, suggests that the
opposite is true. Only when employee empowerment and participation exist does employee ownership appear to have a positive
effect.[110] It may be that empowerment and participation work on
a "real time" basis to show employees that ownership can have
direct and tangible effects.

Ensuring fair pay for performance. Pay policies directly affect
three of the culture elements: rewards for results, fairness (that is,
equity of rewards), and equitable compensation. In Chapter Four
we raised the issue of unfairness when discussing extreme disparities in pay across organizational levels. However, the most
obvious solution, compensation compression, is difficult to act on.
Most American firms are unlikely to adopt a more equitable, let
alone egalitarian, approach to pay just because the Japanese do it.
Compensation compression can have a profound positive effect,
showing employees in a dramatic way the basic fairness of
management. Still, while important, it is probably not a necessary
condition for a TQM culture in most American organizations.

American culture supports strongly the right of an individual to
"rise to the top" and achieve great rewards. It is less important that
management attempts to make compensation more equal than it is
that management makes sure pay is equitable (fair). It is, in fact,
essential that managers show — by their actions — that an
underlying climate of fairness, of equity, exists. This applies to
each of the ten dimensions of fairness defined in Chapter Four.[111]

We have discussed two important ways to demonstrate equity: rewarding results through a formal profit or gainsharing plan, and fostering employee ownership. Programs and policies that strengthen these culture elements will at the same time reduce the negative effect of a relatively large spread in pay from lower to upper organizational levels.

Guaranteeing secure jobs. A surprising number of the best U.S. organizations have formal job security policies, some for many years. It was in 1923 that William C. Procter, then president of Procter & Gamble, *guaranteed* workers 48 weeks of employment a year.[112] Even so, many organizations still resist adopting such policies. This is unfortunate; guaranteed job security is a policy that can benefit the organization as much as it does employees.[113] Providing employees with secure jobs may be the most convincing evidence of management's commitment to TQM. Ensuring job security is a direct, positive response to Deming's injunction to "drive out fear."

Creating a climate of fairness. The concept of fairness incorporates and reflects many of the culture elements identified in Chapter Four. Implementing this concept is not easy, but neither is it impossible. The aim is not sainthood but effective management behavior. Managers must examine their behaviors, the ones shown to relate to the various dimensions of fairness (equity, consistency, fair procedures, etc.). They benefit especially from individual, personalized feedback that shows exactly how others see their actions. This sort of "reality test" enables managers to see their actions more clearly and accurately than ever before. With coaching and trained assistance managers can then make specific changes. Only by changing their behavior, by altering actions that employees see as unfair, can managers create an organizational climate of fairness.[114]

The impact of social tools. We have described some commonly used social/organizational tools. Some of those mentioned are especially important. We included some others because of their widespread use. However, our aim was to provide examples, not to make a comprehensive list of the available social tools. Moreover, in selecting examples we purposely chose tools targeting one or another of the eight culture elements. Each of the eight is directly affected by one or more of our examples.

Job design and the other policies, plans, programs, and practices that we discussed are some of the many social tools that can be used to define organizational climate and culture. These tools may seem "soft" at first glance, but this is not true. They represent major changes in the way managers think and act, just as does TQM. In that sense they are quite "hard," and, sometimes, hard to apply.

Culture, the set of shared beliefs and values that define and direct human behavior in social systems, is created and shaped only by consistent patterns of action. And those action patterns must be carried out over long periods of time. Policies, plans, programs, and procedures can all help define values and beliefs and guide managers in their efforts to make those values and beliefs part of the organization's culture. But, in the end, only practices — actions — count. Neither wall plaques nor positions espoused by top management, no matter how loudly, convincingly, or often, can define or instill values and beliefs. TQM will flourish only when there is "alignment" between what top managers "preach" and what they practice, as seen by people throughout the organization.

Defining a philosophy that embodies a vision and then ensuring that it is reflected in action is the task of leadership. Social tools are useful only in the context of culture–building leadership.

Constructing Culture Through Leadership

In the early 1980s Terrence Deal and Alan Kennedy pioneered in the study of what they called "corporate cultures."[115] They showed how to "read" the culture by looking for symbols and attending to formal and informal activities. These activities — rituals, ceremonies, and traditions, for example — reflect underlying values and beliefs. The stories and "legends" people tell, even the gossip one overhears, can help uncover cultural elements. This is useful when people are loath to (and, perhaps, unable to) speak directly or openly about organizational values and beliefs.

It was tempting to some to skip directly from expressions of culture to the shaping of culture. Some consultants suggested that managers could do so by constructing traditions and ceremonies, by engaging in rituals, and by telling stories that illustrated the values they wanted to "embed" in the organization's culture.[116] But *shaping* culture is very different from *expressing* culture. One organizational psychologist who has studied organizational cultures for years points out that ceremonies, traditions, and other cultural expressions can help clarify and reinforce certain values and beliefs. He goes on, however, to say that these activities probably cannot define those values and beliefs or instill them within the organization.[117] At worst, when overt cultural symbols contradict the values and beliefs that are at work in the organization, management is tarred with the brush of hypocrisy.

In Chapter Four we identified some elements of culture that must be present to support TQM. Policies such as "no layoffs" and programs such as job design help support these TQM culture elements. It is difficult to explain how to use these and other social tools to construct cultural elements, to make changes and make them stick. And, hard as it may be to implement the programs and policies that support TQM, this is *not* the first or the most important step in creating a TQM culture.

Deal and others have, more recently, identified a variety of strategic leadership actions. These actions define and embed values and beliefs within an organization's culture.[118] It is employees' direct experience of the patterns of management behavior and action that defines the values and beliefs that make up the culture, not management-orchestrated symbolism.[119]

Leadership from the very top is what drives TQM. Only when organizational executives — especially the CEO — are absolutely committed to TQM, as a first step, is there a chance for long-term success.   One TQM consultant has observed that while some localized improvements may be possible without top-level commitment, TQM cannot be achieved otherwise.[120]   Only through leadership can the values we have defined and discussed become part of the organization's culture.

How Do Leaders Construct Cultures?

There are three primary types of strategic action that leaders use, more or less in sequence, to construct organizational cultures. First, leaders define a value-based organizational philosophy. Next, they create policies and set up programs based on the philosophy. This is where many of the eight culture elements that support TQM come in. Finally (and, really, all along) they model cultural values and beliefs through their constant and consistent behavior. This may sound like a simple set of one-two-three actions, but it is not. It is the most difficult and complicated set of undertakings related to organizations. Consider in a bit more detail the nature of each of the three types of strategic action.

Defining an organizational philosophy. Leaders start with a value–based vision of what the organization should be, based on and explicitly including TQM values and beliefs. Doing this requires of the leader a level of cognitive capability that is uncommon if not rare. The leader must work with top executives to identify in clear and simple terms just what the organization "is about."

Leaders are not, however, in the business of "selling" their visions. In fact, they rely on others to help identify the essential elements of the vision and values that become the organization's philosophy. They depend especially on other executives but they include others at all organizational levels. When there is a union, top union officials also participate in developing this consensus on organizational values and vision. The process of defining a vision and an organizational philosophy leads to a *shared* vision.

If working with top executives to discuss and define a shared vision seems like a straightforward assignment, consider this description of one such effort by the CEO involved:

> We spent three days. . . . Around the table sat our chief operating officer, the executive vice–president of corporate marketing and development, the vice–president of administration, and me. . . . We sat there hour after hour in an intense debate about the company. We simply could not agree on what Consumers Packaging was and is, never mind what it should be in the future. . . . Here was a group of executives who had been with Consumers for a total of ninety–one years — four people who, I thought, really knew the company. *We didn't have a common language or any way to pro-ceed.*[121] [Emphasis added.]

One reason this CEO and group found their task so difficult is that they jumped into the process of defining a new culture without first looking at where the organization had been and where it now stood. To change an organization's culture, or construct a new one, top managers must begin with a "reading" of the existing culture. This includes its history and current status. A new culture does not suddenly appear out of a vacuum. Cultures are deeply affected by past and present circumstances, and it is foolish to think that one can design a new culture while ignoring the past and the present.

In another case the difficult process of defining the organization's values and philosophy was completed, but the new philosophy did not seem to "take." The cause was opposition, both subtle and overt, from a key senior manager, who could not give up the "old ways." Only after removing this individual from the position of authority in which he could block the executive group's strategy was true consensus achieved. Only then could the group implement the organizational vision and philosophy.[122]

Such difficult and dramatic situations are not always the case. Still, one should not underestimate the difficulty often encountered while developing a meaningful, value–based organizational philosophy. Yet such a shared vision is required to guide and direct policies, programs, and management actions.

Creating policies and implementing programs. Once they have developed consensus among top managers on the values and a vision, leaders define policies and approve specific programs like the ones we described in the previous chapter.[123] These policies and programs support TQM philosophy and action. The best policies and programs create patterns of action that support TQM. Through policies and programs TQM values become part of organizational action in the day–to–day operation of the firm.

Policies that define how rewards are to be allocated are especially important for constructing culture. This is true generally and is especially so with respect to TQM. That is, "rewards for results" is one of the eight culture elements that support the TQM approach. Another crucial policy area is staffing, particularly the hiring of key staff members. Leaders engaged in constructing organizational cultures take great care to select senior staff whose values and beliefs are similar to or consistent with those the leader is trying to inculcate.

In a casual conversation with one of the authors a CEO explained how he had instituted exciting new ceremonies in the organization. His intent was to strengthen the organization's culture, as he had been taught in an executive development program. "What," he was asked, "were your first important actions when you became CEO?" Without hesitation he replied, "Why the first thing I did was to bring on board a few key people who I really knew and could rely on." That is, the CEO chose those people based on values and beliefs that fit with his own and that would support his long-term plans for shaping the organization's culture.[124] Ceremonies and other symbols *reinforce* culture; important task and goal relevant actions (like hiring key staff) *shape* culture.

This is not to say that symbolic factors should be forgotten; quite the reverse. It is important that policies and programs *incorporate* symbolic activities — rituals, ceremonies, etc. Symbols reinforce both values and actions that relate to policies and programs. Consider, for example, a ceremony to present a team with a customer satisfaction achievement award, along with a cash bonus for the team members. The symbolic activity adds an "intangible" meaning to the tangible reward. It strengthens the policy or program, which is now more visible and "real." What's more, the symbolic activity reinforces the values behind the policy. Equity, rewards for results, and authority equal to responsibility are just a few of the values demonstrated by the team's actions and highlighted by the symbolic recognition. It is always important to link tangible work actions and outcomes with intangible symbols and meanings; this is how culture is constructed.

Many of the TQM culture elements we defined can be supported by specific programs and policies. The most important programs are those that empower employees. Thus, job design that makes authority equal to responsibility is one generally useful program. So are TQM tool-based programs (training in the seven old tools, for example) that foster a process measurement approach rather than a results measurement approach.

Policies and programs follow the development of an organizational philosophy and vision. This is because they must be tested in terms of their consistency with the values defined in that philosophy and their contribution to the attainment of the vision. It is through policies and programs that abstractions like values, beliefs, and vision come into contact with organizational reality.

Modeling values and beliefs through leadership behavior. Leaders engage in personal actions that illustrate and reinforce TQM values. This is just as important as defining values and making sure they are reflected in organizational actions. Through these personal actions leaders demonstrate a constancy of purpose. They show their commitment to achieving the organizational vision of total quality management.[125] This is the sort of leadership defined and described by Warren Bennis[126] and practiced by CEOs like Max De Pree (of Herman Miller, the nationally-recognized office furniture manufacturer). De Pree writes, "The first responsibility of a leader is to define reality. The last is to say thank you. In between the leader is a servant."[127]

The CEO of a very large retailing conglomerate was making a tour of a store, encumbered by the usual retinue of vice-presidents, regional and local officials, and miscellaneous attendants. In the midst of a briefing by a vice-president, the CEO noticed a customer wandering down an aisle. He said, "Excuse me for a moment," to the vice-president and walked over to the customer. "Is there something you can't find that I might help you with?" the CEO asked. By his action the CEO strengthened the value of "service to the customer" more than any policy memorandum ever could. In fact, the value probably received more support from this CEO's action than from a year's worth of customer service training.

A recent study of school principals provides another illustration of how leaders define reality and inculcate values by their behavior. The "Experience Sampling Study" was conducted at the National Center for Research and Development on School Leadership (at the University of Illinois). A group of seventy-five principals wore electronic pagers — "beepers" — for a week. The beepers went off at random; each time, the principal was to write down what he or she was doing on a card. At 3:15 p.m. one day the beepers all went off. One principal wrote on his card, "Supervising school bus loading." Across town another wrote, "Encouraging kids to have high achievement goals (as they get on busses)." One principal was acting, quite properly, to manage the school organization. The other was, through her actions, embedding organizational values that would support a TQM culture.

What About the Union?

We noted, in passing, that when there is a union its senior officers must participate in developing the organizational philosophy. They must work along with the CEO and top managers to define values and a vision. This is easy to say but difficult to accomplish, and it is getting harder.

The president of the International Association of Machinists has publicly stated that "it is the policy of the IAM to oppose team concept proposals." He refers in particular to what the IAM calls "the Deming system."[128] The reasons given for this opposition center on the IAM's view that the Deming approach to management does not involve "a real sharing of power between unions and management."

In fact, union-management committees set up to guide the implementation of TQM often do not give the union equal weight in decisions. What is more, the IAM sees the union's ability to veto any proposed action as crucial, but some union-management committees may not permit a union veto.[129] Sometimes these committees have special powers to take actions outside or even in violation of certain terms of the union's contract. At least some union leaders see this as a dangerous precedent that threatens the legitimate authority of the union.[130]

The IAM is not the only union to have open misgivings about TQM. "New Directions," a dissident splinter group within the United Auto Workers union, also opposes union-management cooperation, which they call "jointness." They believe that the auto makers have taken advantage of union "givebacks" and cooperative efforts by eliminating jobs and reducing union power.

As described in a recent book by Joseph and Suzy Fucini, New Directions got its start at Mazda's Flat Rock, Michigan, plant.[131] Mazda agreed not to oppose, indeed to support, unionization in exchange for certain concessions from the UAW. One was to have just two job classifications, production worker and skilled trades, to facilitate greater flexibility. Another was the right to establish its own work rules, without union "interference." The workers were carefully selected and were trained in teamwork and consensus decision making. They were told that they would be involved in designing their work and even in purchasing equipment. So far this sounds like some of the success stories we told in Chapter Four. But reality intervened.

Soon after start up both workers and managers began protesting — and quitting. American managers had expected to manage the plant; they found that they were only expected to carry out the orders of higher-level Japanese managers and executives. Employees had expected to design their own jobs, but they found they were compelled to follow the programmed worksheets provided by Mazda engineers, worksheets that spelled out every step of every job — in detail. There were no purchasing decisions to be made; all the tools and equipment had already been bought and set up in their final places.

In sum, workers found that the plant was closer to an old-fashioned time and motion study-designed system, albeit with self-regulating teams instead of constant and intensive supervision and monitoring. Many employees quit; turnover was much higher than had been anticipated. And when they had the chance, the workers voted out their union reps, despite interference by both the company and the UAW. And so New Directions was born. However, the sources of the greatest problems, the work pace and the high injury rate, were not subject to negotiation due to the original contract agreed to by the UAW.

It should be clear that the conditions at Mazda's Flat Rock plant, as laid out by Fucini and Fucini in their detailed report, bear no resemblance to TQM as we have described it. In fact, the plant design seems to operate on the basis of Frederick Taylor's "scientific management," complete with time and motion study, not on Deming's fourteen points.

There is no doubt that other abuses of the sort outlined here have occurred, sometimes in subtle ways and sometimes almost openly. Recall how some firms saw in quality control circles an opportunity to squeeze a little more out of employees. And in bad times they did not hesitate to lay off many of those who had tried to contribute to improving the organization's products and services. Similarly, some organizations have tried to use TQM and related approaches to reduce union power. This aim often includes increasing management control over workers, and getting more out of employees while reducing costs.[132] Such efforts are certain to fail; people quickly discover such hidden agendas and find creative ways to subvert them. Moreover, it is important to keep in mind that these are *not* examples of TQM; they are perversions of it.

There are two basic ways to guarantee that the sort of threats perceived by union leaders, as defined above, do not materialize. One is to give the union full partnership as equals with management on any labor–management committee. This would include the power to veto any proposed action. The second is to share equitably with employees gains in profit due to TQM–based improvements in quality, performance, and productivity. There must be rewards for these results and this must be a part of the organization's culture. Plans that increase employees' ownership stake based on profitability gains can help.

Trying to "get around" the union, reduce its power, and perhaps even eliminate it, are actions inconsistent with TQM. Such actions make it impossible to create a climate of trust and may actively promote a climate of fear. Without trust, people cannot believe that the principle of equity holds. Fairness will not be an element of the organization's culture. Eventually all the TQM culture elements will be undermined. It is, then, especially important that unions be directly and formally involved in any TQM plans, as full and equal partners.

But what does the union get? To this point we have been discussing union reactions to perceived threats from management, threats that seem to involve TQM. Still, even if management follows our advice and seeks to develop a real partnership with the union, one might ask what benefit there is for the union. Why should unions respond positively and engage in such TQM partnerships with management? It is one thing to "not be attacked" but quite another to identify a positive reason for unions to become involved in TQM.

Our answer is not original, but we believe it to be sound. There is ample evidence that unions must find and fulfill new missions if they are to survive, let alone prosper, in the next century.[133] One way for this to happen is by creating management–union partnerships that develop and support the high level of involvement and cooperation needed for TQM to succeed. Such real partnerships are possible. Both Germany and Japan, two of America's chief economic competitors, have higher levels of unionization than the U.S.[134] And while union membership has decreased by almost half in the U.S. over the past twenty years, it has not changed in Japan or Germany. Writing in the ***Harvard Business Review*** John Hoerr describes how German unions contribute to competitiveness rather than being an obstacle.[135]

Applying such lessons to American industry means that unions must move beyond representation to real involvement. Union leaders, as well as top management executives, will need vision.

For example, in the U.S. joint union–management committees often have special authority to act in ways that would otherwise violate the contract. We have already noted the IAM's objection to such special arrangements. One alternative to special exceptions is to rewrite the contract itself.

This is precisely what union and management did at Shell Canada's Sarnia (Ontario) chemical plant. Management and the Energy and Chemical Workers Union, working together, prepared a new contract to serve as the basis for a vision of joint union–management responsibility. Then they designed a new plant structure. Teams of workers now run the plant, without supervisors. John Hoerr observes, "There is little rule making at Sarnia; instead, labor and management make decisions based on values expressed in a philosophical statement."[136]

Can it happen here? It has. Tom Peters describes how, in the early 1980s, the UAW and Cadillac worked together in Cadillac's Livonia (Michigan) engine plant.[137] Managers, union leaders, and hourly employees were members of a planning team that worked full time for about a year. Together, they came up with plans for the plant's organization and operation. They developed the "Livonia Engine Plant Operating Philosophy." The approach they took emphasizes a partnership between labor and management. It also incorporates the team approach used at Shell Sarnia. All financial records are now open to anyone; there are no more "secret account books" that the union is not permitted to see.

In various ways unions can help keep management honest. Some people, for example, argue that rewards for results, secure jobs, and equitable payment are not crucial elements of TQM. We believe they are. TQM based solely on recognition and other symbolic rewards may seem to be effective, for a time. However, we do not believe that such systems can be sustained over time. Because they have negotiating power, unions can ensure that there are rewards for results and that jobs remain at least as secure as before TQM. Unions may even help spur employee ownership. And they can buck the trend to assume that recognition and symbols are TQM.

John Hoerr identifies several ways unions can exert leverage for positive change. Unions can support new work designs, like the setup at Shell Sarnia mentioned above. Another way that unions can play a positive and important role is by encouraging employee ownership. The United Steelworkers is now involved in ESOPs in 25 companies. And, unions can work with management to take a more active role in employee training. The UAW now runs training institutes in partnership with the auto makers, as does the Communications Workers of America with AT&T.[138]

With a degree of vision on the part of leadership, unions can be the force that tilts the organizational balance toward TQM. Hoerr and others have observed that because the union can say "no," it's choice in saying "yes" can be an important, perhaps essential, factor in driving TQM success.[139] As corporations change, unions, too, must change. This is the essence of a joint, partnership approach to TQM.

Cultural Leadership: Conclusions

Many of the examples and cases we cited earlier involved production or manufacturing organizations. In discussing how leaders build cultures, however, we have purposely tried to give examples from service, sales, and school organizations, all outside the traditional manufacturing arena. TQM and the cultural leadership needed to develop it are applied in much the same way to all types of organizations, not just factories. The tools one uses may appear a bit different in a school, a service organization, or a factory. Still, the TQM values and, for the most part, the cultural elements that support TQM will be the same. And in every case it is culture–building leadership that creates TQM.

Unions have a role to play, too. This role involves much more than simply not acting to obstruct TQM. Union leaders who can participate in defining and constructing a vision, based on a partnership with management, can help create TQM cultures. The need for culture–building leadership is great. Such leadership must come from both union and management.

This leadership commitment means that CEO's and top executives must devote considerable personal time and effort as well as organizational resources to the TQM effort. Some quality consultants claim that quality is free, but it is not. TQM calls for a lot of hard work, along with capital investment. Organizations must commit a variety of resources if they are to implement the changes we have described. Top–level leaders will probably find themselves spending half their time or more on TQM concerns.

One scholar who has researched Japanese organizations for many years reported a conversation with the manager of a Honda engine plant. He asked the manager what he thought of the idea that quality is free. The manager replied, "I could agree with the idea that quality is free these last three years or so. But there were a whole lot of tears for the first twenty years."[140] Quality is not free. In the long run, however, its rewards can be great for all types of organizations.

When put into practice as TQM, through top–level leadership using the strategies described here, the programs, policies, and actions described in Chapters Four and Five will produce a TQM culture. And the results have been demonstrated, repeatedly, to be very positive in terms of long–term organizational effectiveness, that is, profit, performance, and quality.

Recently we asked a publisher of newsletters and some books aimed at managers about his interest in a book proposal. He was pleasant but negative. He explained that his sales of consumer–focused materials were far greater than sales of materials aimed at helping managers improve their organizations. He said, "I'm not sure that managers really want to run their businesses well . . . too [much] hard work."

In the concluding chapter we will look at some evidence to help judge whether our publisher friend was right to be so gloomy. We will also offer some first–step action suggestions for those not afraid of hard work.

Chapter Six

What Does the Future Hold?

In writing this book our aim was to help those who had heard of TQM figure out what the noise was all about. Is TQM just another management fad, or are there some useful ideas there for managers and organizations? While some aspects of TQM (like quality circles) have taken on fad–like dimensions, TQM itself is no fad. TQM has a fifty–year history of success, in the U.S. and Japan.

Another purpose was to help readers make the "right" decision, to pursue TQM for their organizations. Of course, we stated our bias openly to begin with. Many more American organizations must embrace TQM, not as a quick–fix fad but as a serious long–term endeavor. Unless they do America's future as an international economic competitor is dim at best.

While we have spoken often of Japan and Japanese successes in TQM, we have also tried to make it clear, from the beginning, that TQM is an American, not a Japanese, creation. The basic tools were developed by Americans: Shewhart, Deming, Juran, and others. The basic models of a management process and philosophy centered on quality for the customer were developed by Americans: Juran, Deming, and Feigenbaum, among others. And our basic understanding of how culture works and is created was developed by American scholars and practitioners: Parsons, Schein, Walton, and others.

Some elements of TQM culture, like employee ownership, are probably more common in America than in Japan. And we saw that at least one supposed application of TQM by a Japanese firm in the U.S. was clearly not TQM at all. In sum, applying TQM does not mean accepting or adopting elements of Japanese culture, as some who criticize TQM have argued. Of course, neither is it a simple or easy matter.

We hope we have convinced you that difficult as TQM may be, it is less difficult and more desirable than economic failure. But we selected our examples not merely to show that TQM works and has business value. TQM has human value, too. Organizations with TQM cultures are not just more productive and effective, they are far better places for people to work. This is because TQM makes individual — as well as organizational — success more likely, while encouraging conditions that meet human needs at work. TQM is not the lesser of evils; it has great positive value, both for organizations and the people that make them work.

In this final chapter we have two aims. First, we will, as promised in our Introduction, define some first-step actions for those who wish to pursue TQM seriously. Then we will briefly look to the future and the prospects it may hold for TQM.

What First?

Different consultants have developed a wide range of TQM programs. Some are relatively straightforward, with a set of numbered steps and instructions; others are complex, with manuals, charts, and software. Either can work effectively, depending on whether top executives are willing to take the lead in constructing a TQM culture.

We suggest three first steps, but we don't claim that any of them will be simple or easy. Nor will we guarantee that if you follow our advice you will succeed in creating a TQM culture. All we can promise is that if you carry out the following steps you will be ready to begin building a TQM culture — and will, we think, have a good chance of success.

But before jumping into such a project, we suggest that you spend some time thinking about your organization's culture, on your own. Consider whether the values and beliefs that make up the existing culture are in serious conflict with those needed to support TQM. If they are, think twice before starting something that might finish you before you finish it. One reason that it's so hard to change organizational cultures is that they tend to be strong and stable, resisting such change efforts.[141] If TQM values conflict with those that you see in your organization, then you might be better off looking for some other route to organizational improvement.

Step One: Top-Level Leadership Involvement and Direction. Paradoxically, TQM is led from the top, bottom up. That is, TQM works by empowering everyone, especially those at lower levels, and providing them with the knowledge and skills they need to take action commensurate with their work responsbilities. The purpose of such action is to improve quality for the customer. But equally important is leadership from the top, to define and construct a TQM culture. Without cultural support TQM becomes just another program, almost certain to fail in the long run. And *only* leaders can construct such cultures. Thus, the first steps toward TQM must be taken with active, perhaps even vehement, support from the CEO.

If the CEO is not already committed, then the first step must be to develop understanding and active support at the top of the organization. Only then can the following steps succeed. In concept this is simple enough; just educate the CEO and top executive group in the content of this book. If that sounds easy, think again. Top executives aren't usually looking for ways to spend their "leisure hours." And simple attention is not enough. You must also understand the contents of this book well enough to convince the CEO that TQM is worth careful study.

While not easy, getting top–level leaders' attention and interest is not impossible, either. One way is to build many fires. That is, get lots of other people interested. Start a study group yourself. Begin to build a TQM culture in your own area and apply TQM to the extent that you can.

Step Two: A Blue–Ribbon Study Group. Once top leadership makes a real commitment to TQM, the next step is to examine the organization and its culture. The CEO and top executives should be directly involved in a top management–led study group. The group is charged to examine the organization and assess its current fit with and potential for TQM. This should be a careful and serious process of study, not just meetings to jaw over the basic ideas. The group should measure the organization, using both quantitative tools (such as surveys) and qualitative evidence (cultural "artifacts" like traditions, stories, etc.). The group should include people from different parts of the organization and at different hierarchical levels, not just top managers. If there is a union, union leaders must be full members of the study group.

This group is much more likely to succeed with the assistance of an expert outside consultant. The culture of an organization often works to hide important values and beliefs. Sometimes people just don't feel they can talk about these things. Only an outsider can help the study group uncover and come to grips with such facts.

Even when there are no "hidden secrets," we are still subject to blind spots. These are facts of organizational life that we have experienced for so long they seem like a natural part of the organization instead of our inventions. To make an analogy, it is hard for the fish to analyze the water it swims in, the only environment it knows. It is even harder for that fish to understand the nature of "air."[142]

The aim of the study group is not just to increase awareness of TQM. The study group should have three to six months to carry out its assignment: a comprehensive study of the organization, with a focus on its culture and the fit between that culture and TQM. The group's final report will determine whether and how TQM should be implemented. The conclusions of the study group should be formalized in a public final report. If the group's conclusions are positive, suggesting that the organization should pursue TQM, then the study group might also provide recommendations about specific next step actions.

Step Three: An Action Task Force. If the study group report is positive, a long–term task force should be empaneled. Such a task force is often called a "quality council" or has some other TQM–relevant title. It is empowered to develop a TQM plan and begin carrying it out. Top management may have to define a value–based philosophy, as a first step. If a clear philosophy exists the task might be to tie it to organizational operations, through policies, programs and leadership action.

These first, vision–based activities are important. They will make clear the nature of the organization's new commitment to TQM. But many people in the organization are still likely to be skeptical of top management's commitment to TQM. "It's just another program," they will say. Others will feel threatened, especially middle managers who fear that they will lose their control and perhaps even their positions. Only through strong and persistent action on the part of top leaders will those who doubt be convinced and those who fear be reassured.

This task force must, then, take action. That action must directly involve the CEO. Only this will show that TQM is not just another program, that it is a real redirection of organizational action. And only the CEO can both assure mid-level managers that they will not be discarded as powerless leftovers and insist that they support rather than resist or oppose the change.

The action task force will identify specific TQM projects and activities, based in good part on the thorough analysis done by the study group. Because specific actions will depend on what the study group finds and on conditions in the organization, we cannot offer step-by-step suggestions. In general it is important to look at every action proposal in terms of its consistency with a value-based organizational vision centered on TQM. This is when the real work of implementing TQM begins. Our best advice is, as Stephen Covey says, "Begin with the end in mind."[143]

Implementing TQM

Each organization's approach to TQM will be, to a degree, unique. This is because every organization has its own culture, with certain special characteristics that imply specific needs. Moreover, organizations will differ in their applications of TQM simply because it must be the parties themselves that create the plans and actions. Many years ago open systems theorists coined the term "equifinality."[144] It means that there are many different routes to a particular destination. Or, to put it simply, there is more than one way to skin a cat! In the case of TQM the "best" way depends on the preferences of those involved.

Involvement is crucial for success; no outside expert can "install" TQM. Our advice is to run, not walk, away from any expert installer who wants to sell you "the five basic phases of TQM," "the sequence of seven secret steps," or some similar snake oil. Beware in particular of two dangers. First, there are those who would set up a team structure that parallels but does not involve the actual work process of the organization. TQM must be part of the doing of work, not simply an "add–on." Second, watch out for those who suggest that it is all done through a "Quality Assurance Board" or some such high–level group that designs, directs, and implements the entire TQM process. TQM not only requires that everyone be involved, it mandates that everyone be empowered.

Still, we have seen, studied, and participated in enough TQM efforts to know that there are some components that are reasonably generic, common to most if not all. There are three in particular. First, it will hardly be news when we again say that *top level managers must initiate the TQM activity.* Only top leadership can develop a TQM culture. But while TQM is led from the top, it works "bottom–up." Two remaining common components of TQM efforts resolve this apparent paradox.

The second component is a *cross–function team,* composed of managers and employees at different levels and from different parts of the organization. With the help of an outside consultant the team examines and analyzes the organization's culture and work flow systems. These are the sort of activities we had in mind when we described the "Blue Ribbon Study Group" and the "Action Task Force."[145] There might be more than one cross–function team, depending on the size and complexity of the organization. And,

the team might also identify the key processes, inter–unit relationships, and quality problems in the organization (keeping in mind
the Pareto Principle of focusing on the most important 20%).

The third and final common component is *empowering workers and
teams*. This is where the real work of TQM happens: identifying
and solving problems and improving work processes. This may
require modifying or redesigning jobs so that they can be done by
teams.[146] It may also require training, to enable employees and
teams to use their authority effectively.[147] The organization's
culture will almost certainly have to be modified in terms of
policies, programs, and practices that support rewards for results
and other of the culture elements that empower employees.

What Next?

Will it happen? Will American organizations, in meaningful
numbers, begin to move toward real (as opposed to sham or
feigned) TQM? Will we see change in action or only in vocabu-
lary and rhetoric? It is too soon to tell, but there are some positive
indications. Awareness of the importance of quality and organizational interest in TQM are on the rise. Each year more organizations apply for the Malcolm Baldrige National Quality Award.

Survey results show that Juran's and Walton's predictions of the
trend toward self–managing teams are in fact accurate and in
process. The most successful organizations, those in the Fortune
1000, are the ones moving most quickly in this direction.

Finally, consider a recent situation faced by top management of
GM's new Saturn division and the action they took. They discovered that over a thousand cars had been delivered with improperly

mixed chemical antifreeze that could damage the cooling system. Each person who had purchased one of these vehicles was called and asked to return the car and select a new one.[148]

However, there are also some discouraging signs. The desire for quality awards (such as the Deming Prize or the Baldrige Award) has become so great among top managers that incredible efforts have been directed toward winning the award, instead of toward TQM and quality improvement.[149] One result may be the perception among managers and the public of TQM as just another faddish management program.

The Wall Street Journal recently reported the results of a survey of 1237 corporate employees, conducted by Gallup for the American Society for Quality Control.[150] Over 50% reported that their organizations say that quality is a top priority. But only one-third said that their companies followed through on such claims. And less than one-sixth felt that their companies gave them real control over work decisions, an exceptionally important aspect of TQM culture.

It will not be easy for American firms to move all the way to the third, culture-change level of TQM. The first level, use of the tools, is easy (though often a dead end). The second level, an explicit and serious focus on quality for the customer, is more difficult to achieve. It is often attempted only when there is no other option to staunch profitability losses. But unless organizations can move even further and internalize the underlying values and beliefs needed to make TQM effective, the result will be abandonment of the effort and of TQM.

Only through leadership can organizations move to full, culture-based TQM. One well-known organizational psychologist has said it may be that the *only* really important thing leaders do is create organizational cultures.[151]   But he also expressed doubt that leaders of American organizations can make the cultural changes that are needed.   Warren Bennis, who has defined the culture-building strategies leaders use, has also written eloquently of the barriers that potential "visionary" leaders face.[152]

Stephen Covey gives helpful guidance when he observes that to create a TQM culture leaders must begin from the inside out, that is with personal (not simply personnel) changes. Development of character as described by Covey is a process involving considerable work.[153]   He refers to principles involving trust, empowerment, and organizational alignment. These are, of course, aspects of the culture elements we described in Chapter Four.

Despite the difficulties and obstacles faced by leaders who would shape organizational culture, we are optimistic about the potential for success. Both scholars and practitioners know much more about leadership and its dynamics today than was true just a few years ago, thanks to the work of such scholars as Bennis[154] and practitioners like Max De Pree.[155]

We are beginning to understand how leaders construct organizational cultures. There is nothing simple or easy about it, but there is hope that through visionary leadership organizations can be transformed by cultures founded on Total Quality Management.

Some years ago an interviewer asked W. Edwards Deming whether he required a certain number of years commitment from an organization, before he would agree to work with that firm on quality improvement. His answer: "Forever."[156]

NOTES

1. Rensis Likert, *The Human Organization.* New York: McGraw–Hill, 1967.

2. "Business Fads: What's In — And Out." *Business Week,* January 20, 1986. (Page 60.)

3. *Business Week,* op. cit.

4. W. Edwards Deming, "Report to Management." *Quality Progress,* July 1972. (Page 2.)

5. Lester Coch and John R. P. French, Jr. "Overcoming Resistance to Change." *Human Relations,* November 1948. (Pages 512–533.)

6. The academic head of the team was Dr. John R. P. French, Jr., of the University of Michigan. His colleague, Dr. Norman R. F. Maier, introduced the employee team problem solving approach to Detroit Edison in the late 1940s, with considerable success. In one instance a crew assigned to clean coal–fired furnaces redesigned their work process, to the initial opposition of engineers who had designed it as a four–day job and who believed that a worker–designed alternative would take much longer. The crew's new plan cut the furnace down-time from four to two days, an improvement of 100%. The new plan was also far more satisfactory to the crew members themselves. The effect was not short–lived; it held up over time. See Maier's book, *Problem Solving Discussions and Conferences* (New York: McGraw–Hill, 1966), for more details on work group problem solving.

7. The Malcolm Baldrige National Quality Award is sponsored by the U.S. Department of Commerce. In many ways it emulates the Deming Prize. Candidates submit extensive applications, documenting how they meet each of seven major criteria designed to assess how well an organiza-tion has succeeded at total quality management. The criteria used for the Baldrige Award are consistent with and similar to the characteristics of TQM that we will define here. More details on the Baldrige Award can be found in Appendix B.

8. Curiously, it was in this same plant, toward the end of the 1920s and into the 1930s, that the famous "Hawthorne Studies" were conducted. These experiments provided the first formal research on the effects of human relations in organizations. As research experiments the Hawthorne Studies were flawed in very basic and important respects. Even so, they provided the first opportunity for formal, real–life study of the effects of physical and social conditions, including supervisory style and employee participation.

    While Deming was not involved in the Hawthorne Studies, his experiences in the Hawthorne plant impressed on him the need for basic changes in how employees were treated. He concluded, in particular, that piecework — the system of paying a worker only for the number of complete, acceptable items that person produces — was one of the most demeaning and dehumanizing work systems ever invented. In her book *The Deming Management Method* (New York: Putnam/Perigee, 1986) Mary Walton quotes Deming as saying, "Piecework is man's lowest degradation."

    For more information on the Hawthorne Studies see the classic book by the Harvard researcher whose name is most closely associated with this work, Fritz Roethlisberger, and his internal organizational counterpart William H. Dickson, *Management and the Worker* (Cambridge, MA: Harvard University Press, 1939).

9. Shewhart's book, *The Economic Control of Quality of Manufactured Products* (New York: D. van Nostrand, 1931), is still in use. It is the classic work in the field of statistical process control.

10. Deming has said that only about 6% of all problems are due to "special causes," including employee error or failure to perform. The other 94% are, in his judgement, caused by systems — work processes, procedures, and machines — that are often out of control and, as designed, are not easily controllable. Top management designed and put in place these systems and, therefore, the problems they cause are management's responsibility.

    The exact numbers Deming uses to express the proportion of quality problems due to common and special causes have varied over time.

Others put the proportions of common to special causes as 85% to 15% or some other set of numbers. As best we can determine all the numbers, Deming's and anyone else's, are personal guesses, not empirically–determined facts. There appear to have been no formal experiments to see whether Deming's estimate is correct.

It may be true, as some would argue, that employee performance accounts for a much larger proportion of problems than Deming admits. However, this does not change the fact that some proportion, and probably a fairly large proportion, of problems are due to work processes and systems that are out of statistical process control. Current approaches to management typically ignore such problem causes. This makes it impossible to correct many, if not most, quality and performance problems. In contrast, Deming does not ignore problems caused by employees' actions; his approach, and TQM, deal with problems of both types. This is much more important than knowing exactly how much of the overall problem is due to employee error vs. other common and special causes.

11.   The most interesting account of how Deming came to help shape the nature of Japanese industry is told in David Halberstam's book *The Reckoning* (New York: Morrow, 1986). The book tells the story of the decline of the American automotive industry and the corresponding rise of Japanese automakers. In some respects, Halberstam's account differs from that given by Mary Walton in her book *The Deming Management Method* (New York: Putnam/Perigee, 1986), considered by many as the definitive "bible" of the Deming approach.

12.   Deming also donated the royalties from his books, which had become very popular in Japan, to fund the prize. There are actually two major Deming Prize categories, one for organizations and one for the individual who best exemplifies application of quality methods. New categories have recently been established for organizations that have previously won the Deming Prize and for foreign organizations.

13.   In his book, *Dr. Deming: The American Who Taught the Japanese About Quality* (New York: Carol Publishing Group/"A Lyle Stuart Book," 1990), Rafael Aguayo, who took classes from Deming at New York University, observes that Deming "believes every student has

something to offer, something to teach. Deming goes to a class or seminar prepared to learn as well as to teach." (Page xiii.)

14.   W. Edwards Deming, "Report to Management." *Quality Progress,* July 1972. (Page 2.)

15.   Joseph M. Juran, "Product Quality: A Prescription for the West, Part II: Upper–Management Leadership and Employee Relations." *Manage-ment Review,* July 1981. (Page 61.) Quoted in David A. Garvin, *Managing Quality.* New York: Free Press, 1988. (Page 184.)

16.   Some "experts" confuse the two Ishikawa's. The father, Ichiro, was a founder of the Japan Union of Scientists and Engineers, an early chairman of Keidanren, the most powerful association of top business leaders in Japan, and a professor at Tokyo University (Todai), the elite college in Japan from which future industrial leaders invariably graduate. Ichiro Ishikawa was a crucial member of the group of Japanese industrialists who helped foster Japan's industrial recovery through quality. His son, Kaoru, followed in his father's footsteps, becoming a senior official in JUSE, founding the Quality Control Research Group, and writing several important books on quality control and TQM, including the popular English–language book *What Is Total Quality Control? The Japanese Way.* (Englewood Cliffs, NJ: Prentice–Hall, 1985). (Translated by David J. Lu.)

17.   Another of the many formal and informal cultural supports designed to enhance the quality of Japanese products, the powerful Ministry of International Trade and Industry developed and enforces a set of uniform standards for industry called the Japan Industrial Standard (JIS). In the United States there are many organizations that have developed product standards and codes — mostly voluntary (like Underwriters Laboratory, which certifies that electrical products meet defined safety standards). While obtaining the JIS imprint is not, technically, a legal requirement in Japan, the culture–based value of meeting the standard is so strong that most organizations operate as though the standards had the force of law behind them. Japanese manufacturers would not even consider failing to undergo the rigorous review and enforcement procedures defined and overseen by MITI.

18.   This quotation is taken from an interview, "Dr. W. Edwards Deming —
        the Statistical Control of Quality," published in the magazine *Quality,*
        February 1980.

19.   Deming's ideas are presented clearly in a recent book by Mary Walton,
        The Deming Management Method (New York: Putnam/Perigee, 1986).
        A more sophisticated and elaborate presentation can be found in *Dr.
        Deming: The American Who Taught the Japanese About Quality*
        (New York: Carol Publishing Group/"A Lyle Stuart Book," 1990) by
        Rafael Aguayo. To read Deming's own words, see his book *Out of the
        Crisis* (Cambridge, MA: Massachusetts Institute of Technology Center
        for Advanced Engineering Study, 1986).

        Only in very recent years have many American organizations become
        interested in Deming's ideas. More and more, however, have started to
        ask how to attain high quality so as to regain their competitive
        advantage. Thus, in his 90s, Deming continues to maintain an active
        schedule of seminars and consulting assignments that would tax the
        energies of a person half his age.

20.   The titles of the points are, for the most part, as in Deming's book, *Out
        of the Crisis,* while the definitions are based on Deming's most recent
        writing and our interpretation of Mary Walton's descriptions, presented
        in her book *The Deming Management Method.*

21.   Thomas C. Hayes, "Behind Wal–Mart's Surge, a Web of Suppliers."
        New York Times, July 1, 1991. (Pages C1–C2.)

22.   K. Hawley, *Executive Quality Management — What You Get is What
        You Lead.* Minneapolis, MN: Undersea Systems Division, Honeywell
        Corporation, 1989.

23.   It would be foolish to state or imply that Deming's fourteen points are
        the only possible basis for TQM, that nothing else is needed or useful,
        or that all fourteen points are equally important. However, it is equally
        foolish to think that one can pick and choose among the fourteen, using
        only those one likes. This is often what happens when top executives
        hear Deming or read about his approach and decide to begin a TQM
        "program." In such cases the focus is often on those points dealing

with training in the use of statistical tools. The more fundamental, but more difficult to implement, points ("drive out fear;" "eliminate numerical quotas") are ignored. The result is the type of failure we have described in this chapter.

24.   Our descriptions of the seven deadly diseases are based on those given by Mary Walton in *The Deming Management Method.*

25.   They also blame another of Deming's deadly diseases, the mobile manager who is, in their words, "a pseudo-professional," who can supposedly jump from one top-level job to another without any hands-on knowledge or experience of the organization's core production technology or more than the most simple understanding of complex organizational issues. See Robert H. Hayes and William J. Abernathy, "Managing Our Way To Economic Decline." *Harvard Business Review,* July/August 1980. (Pages 67-77.)

26.   Interview with W. Edwards Deming, appearing in *The Wall Street Journal,* June 1, 1990.

27.   W. Edwards Deming, "Report to Management." *Quality Progress,* July 1972. (Page 41.)

28.   Based on comments contained in "Dr. W. Edwards Deming — The Statistical Control of Quality: Part II," published in the magazine *Quality,* March 1980.

29.   Dr. Joseph M. Juran is a contemporary of Deming's. Juran, too, worked in the Western Electric/Bell Laboratories group founded by Shewhart and he also lectured to the Japanese on quality (a few years after Deming's lecture to Keidanren leaders). Juran established an organization to carry out his ideas, The Juran Institute, which delivers public and in-house seminars on quality around the world. He has written many books but the most important is probably his *Quality Control Handbook* (New York: McGraw-Hill, 1951). The most recent edition is called *Juran's Quality Control Handbook* (New York: McGraw-Hill, 1988). A current book by Juran and Frank M. Gryna, Jr., is *Quality Planning and Analysis From Product Development Through Use* (New York: McGraw-Hill, 1989).

Kaoru Ishikawa is best known in the United States for his English-language book, *What Is Total Quality Control?* (Englewood Cliffs, NJ: Prentice-Hall, 1985).

Armand V. Feigenbaum coined the term "total quality control," meaning essentially what we now call TQM, in his classic article, "Total Quality Control" published in the *Harvard Business Review,* November-December 1956. He expanded on this in his book, *Total Quality Control* (New York: McGraw-Hill, 1961).

30. Interview, "Dr. W. Edwards Deming — The Statistical Control of Quality: Part II," published in the magazine *Quality,* March 1980.

31. Quoted in "Talking Business With Juran of the Juran Institute: Value of Quality to U.S. Managers," *The New York Times,* February 6, 1990 (Page D2).

32. See Marshall Sashkin and William C. Morris, *Phases of Integrated Problem Solving.* King of Prussia, PA: Organization Design and Development, 1985.

33. This is one of Deming's fourteen points; see Mary Walton, *The Deming Management Method* (New York: Putnam/Perigee, 1986).

34. There is considerable rivalry among various TQM "gurus" who advocate one or another sophisticated new tool. In his book *World Class Quality* (New York: American Management Association, Membership Publications Division, 1988), Keki R. Bhote argues the inferiority of Genichi Taguchi's "design of experiments" approach as compared with an improved variant developed by his mentor, Dorian Shainin. Bhote rates the gurus, saying

> Phil Crosby is the showman, useful for companies in the dark ages of quality. Juran is superb for general quality management. Deming now concentrates on twisting top management's tail. Shainin alone is the consummate "tool" man . . . a portly man . . . worth his weight in both gold and diamonds . . .

35.   Seiichi Nakajima, *Introduction to TPM.* Cambridge, MA: Productivity Press, 1989.

36.   If this seems uniquely Japanese and culturally inapplicable to the U.S., see William T. Morris' book *Work and Your Future: Living Poorer, Working Harder* (Reston, VA: Reston Publishing Co., A Prentice–Hall Company, 1975; see especially chapter three, pages 96–99). Morris gives examples involving American workers in U.S. organizations, suggesting that a surprising number of Americans have strong emotional attachments to the machines they work with.

37.   David Halberstam, *op. cit.,* page 315.

38.   Warren Brown, "GM–Hughes Marriage Awaits a Spark: Defense Firm's Developments May Be Too High Tech and Too Long Term for Average Car Buyer." *Washington Post,* Sunday April 28, 1991. (Page H1.)

39.   Joseph M. Juran (Ed.), *Quality Control Handbook, Third Edition.* New York: McGraw–Hill, 1974. (Page 2–2.) Juran, more than others, concentrates on concrete ways to implement this concern for what the customer wants, in terms of a systemic quality management process.

40.   W. Edwards Deming, "Report to Management." *Quality Progress,* July 1972. (Page 41.)

41.   Armand V. Feigenbaum, quoted in *Boardroom Reports,* April 1, 1991. (Page 16.) For a more extensive discussion and comparison of various definitions of quality, see David A. Garvin's book, *Managing Quality* (New York: Free Press, 1988). In his article "Competing on the Eight Dimensions of Quality" (*Harvard Business Review,* November– December 1987, pages 101–109), Garvin defines and discusses eight aspects of quality.

42.   Interview with Jeff Maldren of *CBS Sunday Morning,* broadcast of April 28, 1991.

43.   The two are not really in direct competition; the Wegmans store nearest to Stew Leonard's is more than a hundred miles away.

44. Michael Barrier, "A New Sense of Service." *Nation's Business,* June, 1991. (Pages 16–24.)

45. Michael Barrier, *op. cit.,* page 18.

46. Michael Barrier, *op. cit.,* page 19.

47. Michael Barrier, *loc. cit.*

48. Michael Barrier, *loc. cit.*

49. Confidential source, internal to Ford Motor Company.

50. We do not mean to unfairly single out Ford. With the exception of one General Motors Buick model, rated high by consumers in quality surveys, and Cadillac Motors Division, which won the 1990 Malcolm Baldrige National Quality Award, no U.S. automakers compare favorably to the Japanese on either objective quality measures or measures of customer satisfaction.

51. W. Edwards Deming, "Report to Management." *Quality Progress,* July 1972. (Page 2.)

52. Harvey Mackay, best–selling author and CEO of a Minneapolis envelope manufacturing firm, developed a 66–item questionnaire that is used to learn as much as possible about each customer. The questionnaire is not actually sent to customers to complete, but is referred to and updated by employees whenever they contact a customer, to add more information about that customer to the company's file. By learning as much as possible about its customers, the highly successful Mackay Envelope Company is able to respond to their needs better than its competitors. See Mackay's book, *Swim With the Sharks Without Being Eaten Alive* (New York: William Morrow, 1988).

53. "Wal–Mart typifies cooperation between supplier, retailer." *New York Times News Service,* July 14, 1991.

54.   Barnaby J. Feder, "Procter & Gamble designs partnerships to cut costs."
        New York Times News Service. (Memphis Commercial Appeal, July
        14, 1991, pages C1, C10.)

55.   Barnaby J. Feder, *loc. cit.*

56.   Our description of the cycle of quality checkpoints derives in part from
        work by D. Scott Sink and his colleagues at the Virginia Productivity
        Center. See D. Scott Sink and Thomas C. Tuttle, *Planning and
        Measurement in Your Organization of the Future* (Norcross, GA:
        Industrial Engineering and Management Press, 1989).

57.   Yoji Akao and Tetsuichi Asaka (Eds.), *Quality Function Deployment:
        Integrating Customer Requirements into Product Design.* Cambridge,
        MA: Productivity Press, 1990.

58.   Aaron Bernstein, "Quality is Becoming Job One in the Office, Too."
        Business Week, April 29, 1991. (Pages 54–56.)

59.   Joseph M. Juran, *Juran on Planning for Quality.* New York: Free
        Press, 1988.

60.   Reported by Aaron Bernstein, "How to Motivate Workers: Don't Watch
        'Em," *Business Week,* April 29, 1991. (Page 56.)

61.   Aaron Bernstein, *loc. cit.*

62.   Deming estimates that about 94% of all problems, sources of uncon-
        trolled variation, are due to common causes, attributable to the system
        and not to workers. Only about 6% of all problems are due to special
        causes that might be traced to employees. See Deming's book *Out of
        the Crisis* (Boston, MA: MIT Press, 1986) for details.

63.   See Kathleen D. Ryan and Daniel K. Oestreich, *Driving Fear Out of
        the Workplace* (San Francisco: Jossey–Bass, 1991).

64.   This and some of the examples that follow are included in two
        Associated Press articles written by Sharon Cohen and appearing in
        many American newspapers during the week of December 24, 1990.

(The articles can be found, for example, in the Memphis, Tennessee *Commercial Appeal* for December 25 and 26, 1990, pages B10–B11 and B4–B5, respectively.)

65.   For a detailed description of this organization and how its owner and chief executive went about changing its culture, see Ralph Strayer's article, "How I Learned to Let My Workers Lead," *Harvard Business Review,* November–December, 1990. (Pages 66–69ff.)

66.   Tom Peters, *Thriving on Chaos: Handbook for a Management Revolution.* New York: Knopf, 1988. (Page 292.)

67.   Tom Peters, *ibid.*

68.   These examples are detailed in an essay by Ralph Strayer, "How I Learned to Let My Workers Lead," which appeared in the *Harvard Business Review* (November–December 1990, pages 66–69ff). In that article Strayer reviews how, in the course of a decade, he moved the organization's culture from one of authoritarian control to one of employee involvement, based on total quality management. Of course, the sort of changes in decision making described here are just part of the more comprehensive changes Strayer instigated, including changes in the pay system, the appraisal system, and the hierarchy itself.

69.   This is an important point. Simply giving people authority to make decisions and take actions does not mean that their decisions will be good ones or that their actions will be effective. For empowerment to have positive effects, employees must also be *enabled*. That is, they must have the knowledge and skill to use their authority well. This requires training, in TQM concepts and applications as well as in the use of statistical tools for quality control and improvement. Employees will obviously need help to learn how to use control charts or other tools. But there will be other, less obvious, training needs. For example, new teams created to apply TQM methods, either on an ad-hoc task force basis or as permanent work groups, will typically need to learn how to work effectively as a group. This is why Deming emphasizes the need for training (point six) and education (point thirteen).

70.   It is also important that concrete rewards be joined to symbolic rewards. This reinforces the values being rewarded, in an open and obvious manner, making those values stronger and more widespread among the organization's members.

71.   A generally-accepted definition of gainsharing is that it involves sharing with all employees some portion of the gains in performance, productivity, and profit that are achieved as a result of employees' efforts to find ways to do jobs as well or better while reducing costs. The reductions may be achieved by increasing efficiency, reducing waste, or inventing new and better ways to get the job done. All gainsharing plans rely on some concrete, data-based approach to identify (or estimate) the actual gain to the organization from such efforts on the parts of employees. This gain is then shared with employees, often as a bonus, on the basis of a formula that has been agreed on by all parties.

A comprehensive review of the major gainsharing systems used by American firms, including Fein's "Improshare," the Scanlon Plan, and others, can be found in a recent book by Brian Graham-Moore and Timothy L. Ross, *Gainsharing: Plans for Improving Performance* (Washington, DC: BNA Books, 1990). Basic descriptions of two of the most commonly-used plans, Improshare and the Scanlon Plan, can also be found in the following "classic" references:

>   Frederick G. LeSieur and Elbridge S. Puckett, "The Scanlon Plan Has Proved Itself." *Harvard Business Review,* September–October 1969. (Pages 109–118.)

>   Mitchell Fein, "Improving Productivity by Improved Productivity Sharing." *The Conference Board Record,* July 1976. (Pages 44–49.)

72.   Profit-sharing is different from gainsharing. In the former approach employees are simply given some share of the organization's profit, as a bonus, often on an annual basis (as is typical in Japan). There is no attempt to link the amount of profit shared to the savings or profit gain attributable to improvement efforts of employees, as is the case under gainsharing plans.

73. Tom Peters, *Thriving on Chaos: Handbook for a Management Revolution.* New York: Knopf, 1988. (Page 30.)

74. This information from an interview conducted by Garry Coleman, of the Virginia Productivity Center, with Charlie Chandler, CEO of VFC.

75. According to Don Dewar, a well–known quality control consultant, the average American firm with some sort of suggestion system receives about one suggestion for every seven employees, per year. (Dewar was originally cited in *Sales & Marketing Management* and later quoted in the March 15, 1991, issue of the newsletter *Boardroom Reports.*) In contrast, Dewar observes, in Japan Mitsubishi gets about *100* ideas per employee per year, Canon gets *70* per employee per year, and Pioneer Electronics gets *60* per employee per year. It is not, then, uncommon for a Japanese firm to get *six to ten thousand times* as many suggestions per employee per year as do American organizations.

Quality control circles are, at heart, simply small group suggestion systems. In Japan, Musashi Semiconductor (a division of Hitachi Corporation) spent years creating a culture and building the small group skills needed to develop good suggestions. The system went far beyond quality circles. Only after six years was the first group–developed improvement proposal received. During the next year over 26,000 were received, almost 100,000 the following year, and more than double that during the third year. Of the 112,000 improvement proposals submitted during the last six months of the third year of the program, almost 100,000 — 87.8%, to be exact — were implemented.

This was possible because, having built the cultural base for employee involvement and collaboration, the organization did not have to spend a great deal of time carefully examining the proposals to make sure that each one was acceptable to management and consistent with organizational policies; the groups had already done that. Only proposals requiring major capital expenditures or involving other work units need management approval. Despite what appear to be impressive results of this program, the Musashi groups achieved only the *average* when compared with all of the other groups in Hitachi! (See William H. Davidson's article, "Small Group Activity at Musashi Semiconductor Works," *Sloan Management Review,* Spring 1982, pages 3–14.)

76.   This sort of approach works well in a Japanese firm, even though individuals' motivation to attain personal rewards, through individual suggestions, is in conflict with team and quality circle suggestions that result in rewards to all employees as a result of the firms improved profitability. In the (radically) different American culture, the same approach would be a good example of a reward system inconsistency that would surely create problems (assuming that the American organization had both an individually–rewarded suggestion system and a quality circle and/or a gainsharing plan).

          This highlights the need for careful and detailed planning in developing and implementing reward systems. It is much more difficult to develop multi–level reward systems — that operate at the individual, group, and/or organizational levels — than it is to construct systems that function at just one level, be it individual, team, or organization. Japanese organizational culture lessens this difficulty, while American organizational culture makes it even greater. Some would argue that a true TQM system need not include an individual element, but evidence shows that this is not even true in Japan.

          More than a decade ago a Dutch organizational researcher, Geert Hofstede, studied IBM divisions in forty countries around the world. Through a series of surveys he collected a massive amount of data from over 100,000 individuals. Using these data Hofstede identified a set of culture dimensions along which organizations might be compared. On one dimension, individualism, the American part of IBM scored higher than any other unit in any other country. Thus, in the U.S., where the value of individualism is greater than almost anywhere else in the world, it is unrealistic to think that organizations can ignore individual motivation. (For details see Hofstede's article "Motivation, Leadership, and Organization: Do American Theories Apply Abroad?" in *Organizational Dynamics*, Summer 1980, pages 42–62.)

77.   Quoted in an interview that appeared in *The Wall Street Journal*, June 1, 1990.

78.   Some followers of Deming, like Rafael Aguayo (in his book *Dr. Deming: The American Who Taught The Japanese About Quality*), argue that competition is counterproductive whether inside an organiza-

tion or outside. Aguayo opposes all competition, including competition for customers and market. We do not believe that such an argument is viable, simply because the basic economic system in the U.S. will not change from a competitive market basis to a system based on coopera- tion among organizations.

Deming enjoins organizations to teach others, even competitors, and to an extent this idea has taken hold. Many TQM organizations, for example, look to others inside and outside of their own industries to identify "best practices," referred to as "benchmarks." While some organizations refuse to share with others "how it's done," many more are coming to recognize that such sharing is good for everyone and need not be considered proprietary information, to be kept secret in order to maintain the firm's competitive advantage. It is neither realistic nor reasonable to expect American organizations, or American society in general, to abandon competition. It is, however, both realistic and true that organizations are coming to recognize the advantages of collaboration and cooperation, internally and externally. One interesting signal is a recent, widely-publicized agreement between IBM and Apple (reported in *The Washington Post,* July 4, 1991, pages A1 and A28). Instead of continuing their decade-old competition between incompati- ble computers, the two firms have agreed to jointly develop new technology that will permit their future products to use common operating software.

79. Richard E. Walton, "From Control to Commitment in the Workplace." *Harvard Business Review,* March–April 1985. (Pages 76–84.)

80. Joseph M. Juran, quoted in an interview, "Talking Business with Juran of the Juran Institute," in *The New York Times,* February 6, 1990 (Page D2).

81. Quoted by Sharon Cohen, *loc. cit.*

82. Interview with Joseph M. Juran, *loc. cit.*

83. We believe that it is foolish to try to radically change some of the more basic cultural assumptions that are common to American society and reflected in American organizations. Two specific, important examples

are the belief that individuals should be rewarded (equitably) for their achievements, and the value of competition. Culture elements can be moderated and balanced, for example, by developing reward systems that focus on the team and the entire organization as well as on the individual, or by redesigning jobs to make them collaborative team activities rather than work performed by isolated individuals. It is, however, pointless trying to totally reverse existing values and beliefs, for example, by linking all rewards to team and organizational performance or by eliminating competition. Still, some have made impassioned arguments in favor of such radical changes. See, for example, Alfie Kohn's book, *No Contest: The Case Against Competition* (Boston: Houghton Mifflin, 1988).

Instead of trying to radically alter such strong values and beliefs American firms would do better by emulating the Japanese, taking new approaches and integrating them within familiar cultural patterns. This is what Japan has done with respect to Western innovations, beginning in the 1870s, with rapid industrialization under the Meiji emperor, and extending to the present time, with the acceptance of Western political, governmental, and business forms that actually contain within them (sometimes openly and sometimes covertly) very traditional cultural elements. For a good example, see David Halberstam's description of the Japanese recovery after World War II in his book *The Reckoning* (New York: William Morrow, 1986).

84.   In the recession of 1990–1991, when it became clear that "Big Blue" would have to "downsize," a common euphemism for reducing the number of employees, IBM developed a smorgasbord of early retirement and "buy out" packages, but even then no employee was laid off due to economic conditions. Even under the most severe economic conditions IBM has avoided layoffs.

Many organizations are hesitant to make commitments that top managers feel might be impossible to meet. What if, despite the best of intentions, the firm finds no economic alternative to reducing the size of its workforce? One way to deal with this is to make job security an implicit rather than an explicit commitment. Organizations can emphasize that job security depends not on individual assessment but on *organizational* performance. This would seem to be a fairly reasonable point: how can jobs be more secure than the organization? This means, however, that the organization must openly share financial information with employees. Only then can everyone see and understand the economic reality behind "downsizing," should such personnel cuts be required.

85.   Deming sees driving out fear as an especially important aspect of his philosophy of management, emphasizing it as the eighth of his fourteen points. For further details, see Kathleen D. Ryan and Daniel K. Oestreich, *Driving Fear Out of the Workplace* (San Francisco: Jossey-Bass, 1991).

86.   Quality and cost are often thought of as in conflict with one another; the greater the emphasis on quality, the more one increases costs. This, however, is a false assumption. In *The Reckoning* David Halberstam tells of a Ford executive who observed that Japanese auto plants had no areas reserved for reworking defects; they did not need them — as, of course, did American auto factories. This led the executive to rethink the problem and calculate how much could be saved by not having to correct defects, by getting it right the first time. He was astonished to find that the cost of correcting defects was between 20% and 40% of Ford's revenues. The savings obtained by doing the work right the first time would, he concluded, be far more than any possible increase in manufacturing costs. The title of a current popular book by Jeffrey J. Mayer asks, *If You Don't Have the Time To Do It Right the First Time, When Will You Find the Time To Do It Over?* (New York: Simon & Schuster, 1990).

Moreover, as Deming has observed, to assert that increasing quality increases costs is "an argument from ignorance" because only accounted-for costs are taken into account. Other, unknown, costs that may be far more important are ignored, such as the cost of losing a customer due to poor quality of product or service. Greenfield Associates, a licensee of the well-known consulting firm Wilson Learning Corporation, reports that more than 80% of customer losses are due to poor quality of product or service. And, they point out, it costs five times as much to get a new customer as to retain an existing one. In their article "Zero Defections: Quality Comes to Services" (*Harvard Business Review,* September–October, 1990), Frederick R.

Reichheld and W. Earl Sasser, Jr. report that for the various service organizations they studied (including banks, auto repair shops, insurance companies, laundries, and shipping/distribution firms) a 5% decrease in customer "defections" would represent an increase in profit of from 25 to 85%.

These and other issues centered on the falsehood of cost reduction as a strategy for increasing profit are considered by Rafael Aguayo in the first two chapters of his book, *Dr. Deming: The American Who Taught the Japanese About Quality* (New York: Carol Publishing Group/"A Lyle Stuart Book").

87.   Marshall Sashkin and Richard L. Williams, "Does Fairness Make a Difference?" *Organizational Dynamics,* Autumn 1990. (Pages 56–71.)

88.   John A. Byrne, "The Flap Over Executive Pay." *Business Week,* May 6, 1991. (Page 95.)

89.   John A. Byrne, *loc. cit.*

90.   John A. Byrne, *op. cit.,* page 96.

91.   Louis Uchitelle, "No Recession for Executive Pay." *The New York Times,* Monday March 18, 1991. (Pages C1 and C4.) In his recent book *The Work of Nations* (New York: Knopf, 1991) Robert B. Reich shows how the financial disparities between the executive elite and other social class groups in American society has increased dramatically over the last generation and discusses the worrisome implications of this fact.

92.   *Business Week* recently noted that the chairman of UAL, the parent corporation of United Airlines, earned more than $18 million in 1990, while profits fell by 71%. His pay was more than 1200 times that of a new flight attendant — and employees in that category received no pay increases at all from 1985 to 1990. A union official called this situation obscene and immoral.

93.   There appears to be increasing pressure to correct some of the more gross inequities in executive pay in the U.S. This is based on the fact that from 1980 to 1990 corporate profits rose an average of 78%, while CEO pay rose by 212%, almost triple the rate of profit increase. (Worker pay rose 58%, about two–thirds the increase in profitability.) Another reason is that CEO salaries are being reported publicly and widely; the above information and the examples that follow were reported in the cover story of a recent issue of *Business Week* (May 6, 1991, pages 95–112).

The capstone to the argument for limits on CEO pay is concrete evidence that when a firm's profits don't rise — and even when they go down — CEO pay still increases. Lee Iacocca received a 25% increase in total compensation in 1990, even though Chrysler's earnings decreased 79%. The CEO of Reebok, maker of popular tennis shoes, earned over $40 million from 1988 to 1990, including 5% of pretax company profits, while the company's stock appreciated just 17%, with profit up only 1% in 1990 (vs. 1989). In contrast, the CEO of Reebok's chief competitor, Nike, earned about $1 million over the same period, while Nike's return on equity was 23%.

Reebok has a new contract with its CEO limiting his cash income to a maximum of $2 million per year. But putting a limit on executive pay is not done only as a reaction to a negative experience. Herman Miller, a firm noted for excellence (and one we shall speak of again), instituted a policy that the CEO may not receive compensation greater than 20 times the pay of a line employee, conforming to Peter Drucker's guideline.

94.   Harvey Mackay, *Swim With the Sharks Without Being Eaten Alive.* New York: William Morrow, 1988. (Page 191.)

95.   Michael Conte and Arnold S. Tannenbaum, *Employee Ownership.* Ann Arbor, MI: Survey Research Center, Institute for Social Research, The University of Michigan, 1980.

96.   Richard L. Williams helped draft this discussion of the nature of culture.

97.   Job design is sometimes referred to as "job redesign" or "job enrich-
        ment." It always involves giving workers greater control over their own
        work actions. The job is usually defined (or redefined) so that the work
        activities of an employee (or a team) make up a "whole" or more
        coherent and complete task. Typically, employees are also given the
        authority to make and implement work–related decisions when such
        decisions do not directly affect other employees or work groups.

        The pioneer of job enrichment is Frederick Herzberg. For details see
        his classic *Harvard Business Review* article, "One More Time: How Do
        You Motivate Employees?" (January–February 1968, pp. 53–62). This
        is one of the most requested and reprinted articles *HBR* has ever
        published.

98.   This definition combines three elements. The first is what we called
        enabling conditions (in Chapter Four). The second element is job
        design. The third is what we referred to as empowerment. For more
        details, see Kenneth W. Thomas and Betty A. Velthouse, "Cognitive
        Elements of Empowerment." *(Academy of Management Review,*
        October 1990, pages 666–681.)

99.   M. D. Kilbridge, "Reduced Costs Through Job Enrichment: A Case."
        The Journal of Business, 1960, volume 33, pages 357–362.

100.   William J. Paul, Jr., Keith B. Robertson, and Frederick Herzberg, "Job
        Enrichment Pays Off." *Harvard Business Review,* March–April, 1969.
        (Pages 61–78.)

101.   Marshall Sashkin, *Making Participative Management Work.* King of
        Prussia, PA: Organization Design and Development, Inc., 1989.

102.   Richard E. Walton, "How to Counter Alienation in the Plant." *Harvard
        Business Review,* November–December, 1972. (Pages 70–81.) For a
        more recent look back at this case, see Walton's article, "From Control
        to Commitment in the Workplace," in *Harvard Business Review,*
        March–April, 1985. (Pages 76–84.)

103.   Rollin Glaser, *Moving Your Team Toward Self–Management.* King
        of Prussia, PA: Organization Design and Development, 1990.

104. Richard E. Walton, "From Control to Commitment in the Workplace." *Harvard Business Review*, March–April 1985. (Pages 77–94.)

105. Marshall Sashkin and William C. Morris, *Organizational Behavior: Concepts and Experiences*. Englewood Cliffs, NJ: Reston Publishing Company/"A Prentice–Hall Company," 1984. (Chapter 11, Job Design.)

106. Chris Argyris makes this point in detail in his classic book *Personality and Organization* (New York: Harper & Row, 1957).

107. David C. McClelland has researched this basic human motive for many years. A good summary of his results can be found in his book, *The Achieving Society* (New York: Irvington, 1976). In an earlier book McClelland shows how the achievement motive can be developed and organizationally supported. See David C. McClelland and David G. Winter, *Motivating Economic Achievement* (New York: Free Press, 1969).

108. The human need for task–related (not simply "social") interaction at work is best expressed in the research and writings of those involved with the "socio–technical systems" approach to the study of organizations. See William A. Pasmore and John J. Sherwood, *Sociotechnical Systems: A Sourcebook* (San Diego, CA: University Associates, 1978).

109. Marshall Sashkin, *Making Participative Management Work*. King of Prussia, PA: Organization Design and Development, Inc., 1988.

110. A major research study involving forty–five firms with some form of employee ownership concluded that employee ownership plans lead to high satisfaction and outstanding organizational performance when employees have "participative opportunities on the job." See Corey Rosen, Katherine J. Kline, and Karen M. Young, *Employee Ownership in America: The Equity Solution* (Lexington, MA: Lexington Books, 1986). Similar findings were obtained in an earlier research study involving three firms in the northeast U.S. and western Canada. See Richard J. Long, "Job Attitudes and Organizational Performance Under Employee Ownership." *Academy of Management Journal*, December 1980. (Pages 726–737.)

111.   Many people incorrectly assume that *equality* is the same as *equity*.
        Equity, which is crucial for TQM, means that people agree that rewards
        (or punishments) are allocated in the same way to everyone. For
        example, if one person's job is twice as hard as another's, it would be
        equitable for the first person to be paid twice as much. So, even though
        some people receive greater rewards than others, the situation is
        equitable if it is generally agreed that those individuals have acted in
        ways that demonstrate their unequal rewards are deserved. A complete-
        ly equitable system can easily result in very unequal allocation of
        rewards, because equitable rewards are based on the value one adds to
        the organization through one's actions, activities, and products.

112.   Mitchell Fein, "Job Enrichment: A Reevaluation." *Sloan Management
        Review,* Winter 1974. (Pages 69–88.)

113.   In his book *Dr. Deming, the American Who Taught the Japanese
        About Quality* (New York: Carol Publishing Group/"A Lyle Stuart
        Book," 1990), Rafael Aguayo contrasts the responses of Chrysler and
        Mazda when faced by financial difficulties. At Chrysler CEO Lynn
        Townsend fired many engineers. Costs were dramatically reduced and
        the balance sheet improved — in the short run. But soon the firm was
        in even worse shape; it required massive infusions of funds borrowed
        from the Federal Government to save Chrysler. At Mazda not a single
        engineer was laid off. Many, however, were given new assignments,
        including work as salesmen in dealers' showrooms. When conditions
        improved a few years later the engineers who had been assigned to
        sales returned with incredibly valuable new insights as to customers'
        needs. They could apply their learnings directly, to design and
        engineering activities. While Chrysler was asking for protection and
        Federal loans, Mazda was experiencing a boom.

114.   Marshall Sashkin and Richard L. Williams have developed a variety of
        assessment and training materials to help managers determine the
        climate of fairness in their organizations and then improve it. See
        Marshall Sashkin, *The Managerial Mirror,* and Richard L. Williams,
        The Managerial Mirror Participant Workbook, both published by and
        available from Organization Design and Development, Inc. See also
        Marshall Sashkin and Richard L. Williams, "Does Fairness Make a
        Difference?" *Organizational Dynamics,* Autumn 1990. (Pages 56–71.)

115. Terrence E. Deal and Alan Kennedy, *Corporate Cultures.* Reading, MA: Addison-Wesley, 1982.

116. For examples of how consultants have flocked to work in the field of organizational culture, see Bro Uttal's report, "The Corporate Culture Vultures," in *Fortune* (October 17, 1983; pages 66-72).

117. Edgar H. Schein, "Organizational Culture," *American Psychologist,* February 1990. (Pages 109-119.)

118. Terrence E. Deal and Kent D. Peterson, *The Principal's Role in Shaping School Culture.* Washington, DC: Government Printing Office, 1990.

Marshall Sashkin and Molly G. Sashkin, "Leadership and Culture-Building in Schools: Quantitative and Qualitative Understandings." Paper presented as part of a symposium at the annual meeting of the American Educational Research Association, Boston, April 20, 1990. (ERIC Document ED 322 583.)

119. Culture is quite stable and can be very hard to change. Brian Dumaine tells a story in his article, "Creating a New Company Culture" (in *Fortune* magazine, January 15, 1990), about a consultant hired by a Fortune 500 manufacturer. The consultant was asked for help with a plant that had a history of poor labor relations and low productivity. He interviewed employees, who told him about "Sam," the plant manager. Sam was as big as a gorilla and had a temper much worse. Sam had once taken a sledgehammer and personally demolished a product he didn't like the looks of; another time he drove his car *into* the plant, climbed on the roof, and screamed at the workers. The consultant was horrified but assumed he now knew the cause of the plant's problems. He finally screwed up his courage and went to see the plant manager, but behind the desk was an ordinary-looking fellow named Paul. Asked where Sam was, Paul said, "Sam's been dead for nine years." Paul and the consultant spent four years undoing Sam's cultural legacy.

120. Joseph R. Jablonsky, *Implementing Total Quality Management.* Albuquerque, NM: Technical Management Consortium, 1990.

121.   Benjamin B. Tregoe, John W. Zimmerman, Ronald A. Smith, and Peter
        M. Tobia, *Vision in Action: Putting a Winning Strategy to Work.*
        New York: Simon & Schuster, 1989. (Pages 37–38.)

122.   Mark A. Frohman and Marshall Sashkin, "Achieving Organizational
        Excellence: Development and Implementation of a Top Management
        Mind Set." Paper presented as part of a symposium, "Achieving
        Excellence," at the annual meeting of the Academy of Management, San
        Diego, August 1985.

123.   We use the term "policy" to mean a statement, usually in writing and
        public, that tells how the philosophy applies to a specific organizational
        practice, such as staffing, purchasing, or dealing with customer
        problems. For example, a staffing policy might explicitly state that
        hiring decisions must take into account the extent to which candidates
        exhibit through their past actions the values that are crucial to the
        organization's philosophy. A purchasing policy might define the
        parameters under which employees are expected to make purchase
        decisions without higher–level approval, thus explicitly supporting their
        empowerment in this respect. A policy centering on customer problems
        might state that customer service staff have full authority to make
        whatever adjustment they decide is appropriate, based on the company's
        commitment to quality for the customer.

        A program usually refers to a special, planned set of activities,
        sometimes with a starting and an ending date. Programs, like policies,
        put into action the organization's philosophy and the values that define
        that philosophy. There might, for example, be a special program to
        train employees to collect information to assess customer problems and
        to make data–based decisions about what corrective actions to take.
        Such a program might be important if the customer problem policy just
        mentioned is to work well. Programs often support or put into action
        certain policies. And both policies and programs express the values on
        which the organization's philosophy is based.

124.   We don't mean to suggest that to change cultures CEOs always begin
        by replacing top managers. Often, individuals with supportive values
        will be found within the organization, if not in particular or "key"
        positions. Our point is that leaders who build cultures look for such

individuals, whether within or outside of the organization, and use them to support the leaders' values, philosophy, and vision.

125. This form of leadership is described in more detail in Marshall Sashkin, *Becoming A Visionary Leader.* King of Prussia, PA: Organization Design and Development, 1986.

126. Warren Bennis and Burt Nanus, *Leaders: The Strategies for Taking Charge.* New York: Harper & Row, 1985.

127. Max De Pree, *Leadership Is an Art.* New York: Doubleday, 1989. (Page 8.) Herman Miller was founded in 1923 by Max De Pree's father. The firm pioneered in quality design and manufacture of office furniture. The Eames chair, named for its designer, Charles Eames, is a good example. Samples are in the permanent collection of the New York Museum of Modern Art and the Louvre, in Paris, as examples of classic design. Most, if not all, of the TQM culture–building factors described here have been in place at Herman Miller for generations — the Scanlon Plan since 1952, a participative management approach and employee stock ownership plan almost as long. Herman Miller is considered one of the 100 best companies to work for in America. James O'Toole reports that over the decade from 1975 to 1985 Herman Miller stock had a compound annual growth rate of 41 percent. Recently ranked 456th in total sales by *Fortune* magazine, Herman Miller was at the same time ranked *seventh* among the Fortune 500 in total return on investment over ten years.

128. George Kourpias, president of the International Association of Machinists, issued a "white paper" in the fall of 1990, setting forth the union's policy views. In his accompanying letter to union officers Mr. Kourpias wrote, "These programs by their very nature interfere with our duty to protect the interests of all bargaining unit members." These and further details are reported in an article by Frank Swoboda, "Union Leader: Managers Pull the Strings in 'Team' Programs," appearing in the *Washington Post,* Sunday, April 14, 1991.

129. This applies as well to other organizational change and improvement approaches — such as self–directed teams, quality of work life, and employee participation — that involve management–union committees.

130.   More subtly, union leaders may fear that successful TQM will reduce or remove the need for the union, since management voluntarily gives employees benefits (such as more meaningful jobs, greater autonomy, and increased authority) as well as sharing profits derived from productivity and performance gains and quality improvements. These outcomes would otherwise be obtainable only through union negotiation.

The IAM proposes to avoid this problem by approving only of programs that are based on "the structural exclusion of management from a direct relationship with the rank and file." It is the IAM's position that this will ensure that the union will not be "bypassed" by management. For additional details see Frank Swoboda's article, *op. cit.*

131.   Our summary of this case is based on the report of Joseph J. Fucini and Suzy Fucini in their book, ***Working for the Japanese: Inside Mazda's American Auto Plant*** (New York: Free Press, 1990).

132.   Some believe that this is the only underlying purpose of TQM and team concepts. In their book, ***Choosing Sides: Unions and the Team Concept*** (Boston: South End Press, 1988), Mike Parker and Jane Slaughter argue that the intent of TQM is to "stress the system" so as to identify weak links, such as a few seconds of "wasted" time, and then "correct" them. This forces workers to perform at their maximum level of effort, until they literally burn out. We do not agree that this is part of any sound TQM approach. While the sort of abuses detailed by Parker and Slaughter, and by Fucini and Fucini, have no doubt occurred, we see them as perversions of TQM, not as typical examples.

133.   For an excellent overview and current discussion see the article "What Should Unions Do?" by John Hoerr, in the *Harvard Business Review,* May–June 1991. (Pages 30–45.) Many of the ideas in the discussion that follows are based on specific concepts and concerns identified by Hoerr.

134.   John Hoerr, *op. cit.*, page 30.

135.   John Hoerr, *op. cit.*, page 37–39.

136.   John Hoerr, *op. cit.*, page 42.

137.   Tom Peters, ***Thriving on Chaos.*** New York: Knopf, 1987. (Pages 297–298.)

138.   John Hoerr, ***loc. cit.***

139.   This point is made in an article by economists Adrienne E. Eaton and Paula B. Voos, in ***Unions and Economic Competitiveness,*** edited by Lawrence Mishel and Paula B. Voos (New York: M. E. Sharpe, 1991) and cited by John Hoerr, ***op. cit.***, page 39.

140.   Robert E. Cole, "Large–Scale Change and the Quality Revolution." In A. M. Mohrman, Jr., S. A. Mohrman, G. E. Ledford, Jr., T. G. Cummings, and E. E. Lawler, III (Eds.), ***Large–Scale Organizational Change.*** San Francisco, CA: Jossey–Bass, 1990.

141.   Remember Sam, the plant manager. The culture he created lived on long after he had died.

142.   This concept was first stated by Marshall McLuhan in his classic text ***Understanding Media*** (New York: McGraw–Hill, 1964).

143.   Stephen R. Covey, ***The 7 Habits of Highly Effective People.*** New York: Simon & Schuster, 1989. (Pages 96–144.)

144.   Daniel Katz and Robert L. Kahn, ***The Social Psychology of Organizations.*** New York: Wiley, 1966. (Chapter One.) (Revised edition, 1978.)

145.   These actions might be the province of the study group. The task force might concentrate more on identifying key processes and on planning and implementing a work team approach. But remember, there's more than one way to skin that cat!

146.   While a team approach to work design is common — and powerful — we don't mean to imply that it is always required. There are situations that call for individual work design, and there are individuals whose clear preference is to work alone rather than in a team. In general, it seems that the team approach is becoming the most common form of job design, both in traditional industries and in "post–industrial" high

technology settings. Enablement and empowerment *are* absolutely crucial, in all contexts; team work design is not.

147.   Organizations often overspend for training, providing extensive workshops that cover more statistical tools and techniques than employees need or can use. This is especially true when the organization mistakenly confuses tools and techniques with TQM, but it can happen even when the TQM efforts are correctly focused. Effective training meets the needs of "customers," that is, the trainees. It is designed to address specific needs of participants. And, such training typically takes place in the work context, not in a classroom or off–site.

For example, if team members need to learn to work together more effectively, the appropriate training approach would involve a training consultant meeting with the team to examine and deal with specific problems they have. If individuals need to learn to use certain tools for collecting data and analyzing problems, they can best do so through guided practice involving their actual work. Effective TQM training is not "pantyhose" training where one size fits all.

148.   This event was widely reported in May, 1991, when Saturn's management publicly announced both the problem and the action taken by the company. Saturn is General Motors' new "nameplate" and division created specifically to challenge the Japanese by building an inexpensive small car of very high quality. Auto industry experts believe that in its first model year (1991) Saturn cars are as good as any Japanese–built autos in their price range. Built in Spring Hill, Tennessee, in a new plant designed from the ground up, Saturn was given considerable autonomy from the GM bureaucracy. Both the latest technology and the principles of TQM culture are basic to the Saturn organization.

149.   Florida Power and Light devoted years of very costly effort to winning a foreign–organizations version of the Deming Prize. A recent magazine article, however, pointed out that the organization is now in financial trouble, that it's customer satisfaction record is now worse than other Florida utilities, and that the CEO and vice–president for quality had to be removed as a result of the debilitating prize–oriented efforts. FP&L, said *Fortune*, had been pushed close to the organizational version of a nervous breakdown (reported in the July 1, 1991, issue).

150. "Quality Programs May Be Shoddy Stuff," in the column *Managing* by Amanda Bennett, appearing in the *Wall Street Journal,* October 10, 1990.

151. Edgar H. Schein, *Organizational Culture and Leadership.* San Francisco, CA: Jossey–Bass, 1985.

152. For a detailed description of how leaders act strategically to build culture, see Warren Bennis and Bert Nanus, *Leaders: The Strategies for Taking Charge* (New York: Harper & Row, 1985). On the problems faced by leaders, see Warren Bennis, *Why Leaders Can't Lead: The Unconscious Conspiracy Continues* (San Francisco: Jossey–Bass, 1989).

153. Stephen R. Covey, *The 7 Habits of Highly Successful People: Restoring the Character Ethic.* New York: Simon & Schuster, 1989.

154. Warren Bennis, *On Becoming a Leader.* Reading, MA: Addison–Wesley, 1989.

155. Max De Pree, *Leadership Is an Art.* New York: Doubleday, 1989.

156. Quoted in an interview with Dan Gottlieb published in the *Washington Post,* January 15, 1984 (Page D3).

Appendix A

The Seven Old Tools

The seven old tools are very basic, but very important. Deming's thirteenth point states that everyone must learn the basics of statistical theory and application, since this is the language of improvement. We have already referred to some of the seven tools; let us very briefly define each one.

Control Charts. These charts display the results of statistical process control measures. They show whether product samples conform to specified limits or tolerances. Control charts give a

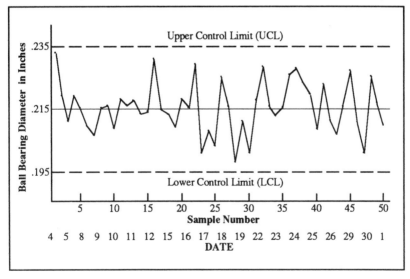

Figure A: Control Chart

clear visual display that quickly tells one when a process is "out of control." When random sampling yields measurements above the upper control limit or below the lower control limit, this triggers a search for the cause of the problem. The production process can then be corrected and brought back "into control." Control charts are important and basic statistical process control tools.

Pareto Charts. This is an even simpler tool, used to chart the number of defects or problems of various types in a product over time. One simply counts the number of problems or defects of each type, over time. The results are displayed on a chart as bars of varying length. The underlying principle, based on the work of the nineteenth–century Italian economist Vilfredo Pareto, is that about 80% of all problems can be traced to only 20% of all the varied possible causes; the remaining 80% of causes account for only 20% of the problems and defects.

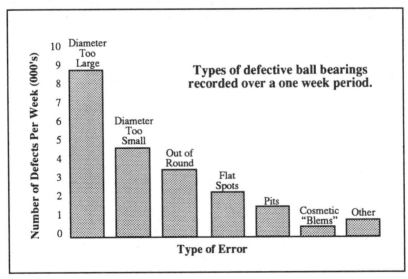

Figure B: Pareto Chart

This means that to get the most out of improvement efforts one should always begin by attacking those few causes that are responsible for the majority of all quality problems. A Pareto chart can help identify the relatively few categories of causes that account for most problems. The chart can also be useful for identifying points in the production process at which defects of certain types are most likely to occur.

Fishbone Diagrams. These are also called "cause and effect diagrams" or Ishikawa diagrams (after Kaoru Ishikawa, who first developed this tool). The chart looks somewhat like a fishbone, with the problem or defect — the "effect" — defined at the "head." On the bones growing out of the spine one lists possible causes of production problems, in order of possible occurrence. The chart can help one see how various separate problem causes might interact. It also shows how possible causes occur with respect to one another, over time, helping start the problem solving process.

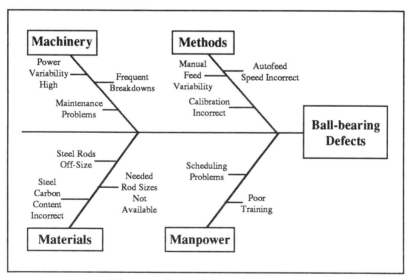

Figure C: Fishbone Diagram

Run Charts. These forms, sometimes called "trend charts," are used to display measurements made over specific time intervals — a day, a week, or a month, for example. One can then construct a graph, with the quantity measured on the vertical axis and time along the horizontal axis. A run chart is, then, little more than a running tally. Its major use is to help figure out whether there are critical times during problems of various types occur. One can then investigate why this is so.

For example, a plot of defects by hour or day might show that problems consistently appear when materials from a certain supplier are used (as on July 11 in Figure D, below). This suggests that materials from that supplier might be the cause. Or, it may be found that a specific machine comes on line at the same time that certain problems appear, suggesting that the cause might be something wrong with that machine.

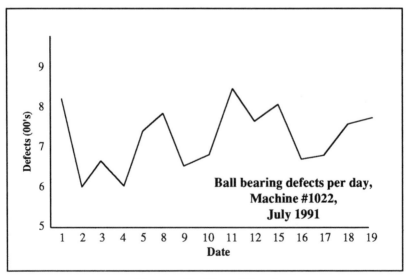

Figure D: Run Chart

Histograms. A histogram is also known as a "bar chart." On this chart the number of products in each "control category" (that is, at each of a number of separate, measured values) is represented by the length of a bar. Each category is labelled and the bars are placed next to one another, horizontally or vertically. This shows which categories account for most of the measured values as well as the comparative size of each category. Histograms give a picture of the actual distribution of measures. They can show whether or not the distribution is "normal" (shaped roughly like a bell).

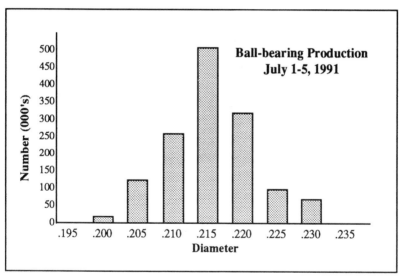

Figure E: Histogram

Scatter Diagrams. These diagrams provide a standard way of showing how one variable, for example, tensile strength of a wire, relates to another, such as the wire's diameter. In this example the strength of wire of various diameters would be tested by pulling on the wire until it broke. The exact strength required to break each wire would be recorded. The results would then be graphed, diameter on the horizontal axis and strength on the vertical. It would then be possible to see clearly the relationship between wire tensile strength and wire diameter. This sort of information is useful for product design.

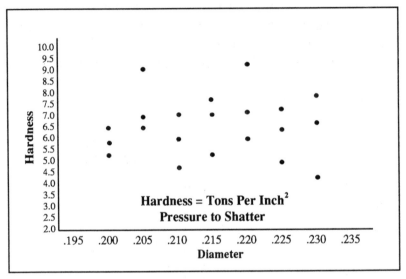

Figure F: Scatter Diagram

Flow Charts. Flow charts, sometimes called input–output charts, give a visual description of the specific steps in a work activity. This can be extremely helpful for understanding exactly how things are being done and then determining how a process might be improved. The procedure can be applied to the entire organization, too, to visually track and chart the way the organization operates.

Flow charts use certain standard symbols to refer to certain types of activities (such as decisions, shown by diamonds, and activities, shown by boxes) but these conventions are not as important as getting down a clear description of the sequence of work activities. Flow charts can also be used to design improved work processes, by showing how things *should* happen and comparing this with the way things actually do occur.

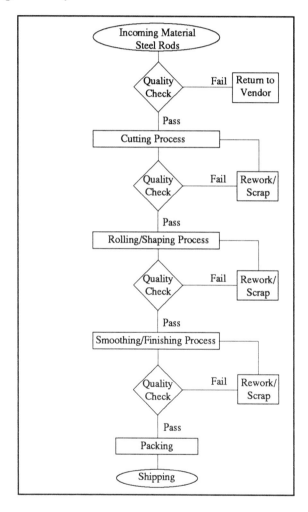

Figure G: Flow Chart

Appendix B

The Baldrige Award[*]

The Malcolm Baldrige National Quality Award was established by a 1987 act of Congress. Up to two awards are made annually in each of three categories: manufacturing, service, and small business. The purpose is to recognize U.S. companies that excel in quality achievement and quality management. While modeled on the Deming Prize, the requirements and procedures are not identical.

Applicants submit extensive, detailed documentation as to their qualifications with respect to each of seven major "Examination Categories." Each of the seven categories has two or more sub-criteria or "items," with 28 specific items in all. Each category and each item in a category is assigned a certain point value, based on importance. Items are valued from 15 to 75 points, while the seven categories range from a low of 60 points to a high of 300.

---

[*]Most of the information contained here is quoted or adapted from the *1992 Application Guidelines: Malcolm Baldrige National Quality Award.* Single copies of the latest *Guidelines* are available at no cost from:

>Malcolm Baldrige National Quality Award
>National Institute of Standards and Technology
>Gaithersburg, MD 20899
>(Telephone: 301 975-2036; Fax: 301 948-3716).

Substantial fees are required of organizations that submit applications judged eligible to compete. For 1992 the charge is $4000 for manufacturing and service firms and $1200 for organizations in the small business application category. These fees cover only the costs of application reviews. There are additional charges for the site visit reviews conducted for the relatively small number of applicants that successfully accomplish the first two stages of the review process.

Applications are first reviewed by a panel composed of four members of the 150–person Board of Examiners. The Board members are quality experts selected from business, professional and trade organizations, accrediting bodies, universities, and government. Individuals apply for membership through a rigorous selection process. They then complete an examination preparation course that ensures a thorough understanding of the examination process, the specific items, how to use the scoring system, and how to prepare feedback reports.

There are three types of Board members: Examiners, Senior Examiners, and Judges. The first review panel is composed of at least three Examiners and a Senior Examiner, who leads the group. Their report is read by the Panel of Judges, which determines whether the application goes on to the second stage, called "Consensus Review."

This second review is similar, with a new group of at least three Examiners and a Senior Examiner group leader. This time, the Panel of Judges reviews the report to decide which applicants receive site visits.

The site visit review is conducted by at least five members of the Board, led by a Senior Examiner. They visit the applicant's facilities and operating units, review records and data files, and interview corporate officials. They report their findings to the Panel of Judges.

The Panel of Judges reviews all of the site visit reports and makes recommendations as to which applicants should receive awards. The National Institute of Standards and Technology receives these recommendations and presents them to the U.S. Secretary of Commerce, who makes the final decisions. After the awards have been announced, all applicants receive extensive feedback reports.

Examination Categories and Items

The chart below shows the seven categories and the point value for each. The seven are broken down further into two to eight sub-categories or "items," with each item having a specific point value (the 28 items are not shown on our chart).

Baldrige Award Criteria and Point Values		
1.0	Leadership	90
2.0	Information and Analysis	80
3.0	Strategic Quality Planning	60
4.0	Human Resource Development and Management	150
5.0	Management of Process Quality	140
6.0	Quality and Operational Results	180
7.0	Customer Focus and Satisfaction	300

The most important examination category is "Customer Focus and Satisfaction." This supports one of the central points of this book, that is, the fact that the whole aim of TQM is quality for the customer. Customer Focus and Satisfaction counts for 300 points, twice as much as any other examination category.

Three other examination categories are considered very important, at 140 points or more: "Quality and Operational Results," "Management of Process Quality," and "Human Resource Development and Management."

The Quality and Operational Results category involves what we called "results metrics" in Chapter Five, but this does not refer just to inspection (Quality Checkpoint 2). Measures of the quality of results are taken at QC3, QC4, and QC5, as well as QC2. These measures, however, are at the organizational level and do not reflect on individuals or identifiable work teams. This examination category is intended to provide comprehensive measures of the absolute level of quality obtained throughout the organization, in terms of results and outcomes.

Management of Process Quality refers to "process metrics" at QC2, QC3, QC4, and QC5. Each quality checkpoint is assessed by one or more of the specific items in this category. (Recall that QC1 is covered primarily by the customer satisfaction category.)

The Human Resource Development and Management category includes some of the eight TQM culture elements defined and discussed in Chapter Five and Chapter Six. For example, "employee performance and recognition" (rewards for results) counts for 25 points, while "employee involvement" (authority equal to responsibility) is worth 40 points. While a number of the items that make up each examination category relate to one or more of the eight TQM culture elements, the connections are generally indirect and implicit rather than clear and explicit, as for the two examples just cited.

In Chapter Six we discussed the importance of top–level leadership for constructing a TQM culture. The examination category "Leadership" counts for 90 points. Thus, the Baldrige Award does recognize that leadership has an explicit role to play in TQM, even though in our view the point value placed on leadership is a serious underestimation of its real importance.

The examination category "Strategic Quality Planning" also examines culture, asking whether there is a comprehensive organizational philosophy based on TQM. The category also includes items that assess whether this TQM philosophy is implemented through long–term planning, strategy development, and tactical implementation. The category as a whole is given a total of 90 points.

"Information and Analysis," the examination category with the least total points — just 60 in all — refers to the tools we described in Chapter Three. (Training for organization members in the use of the tools is assessed by an item included as part of the Human Resource Development and Management examination category.) The value assigned to Information and Analysis supports our view that tools, techniques, and training – while not unimportant — are actually the least crucial aspect of TQM.

TQM and the Baldrige Award

Even the brief review given above should make it clear that in concept the Baldrige Award is consistent with the view of TQM proposed in this book. What differences exist are for the most part differences of emphasis, not substantial or substantive areas of conflict.

We feel obliged, however, to add a word of advice: before deciding to pursue the Baldrige National Quality Award, top executives should reflect thoughtfully on their motives for doing so. The effort and the actual costs involved in competing for the Baldrige Award can be very great. While it may seem tempting to "go for" the Baldrige to demonstrate to others the organization's quality orientation, this is actually a poor reason for applying. Firms that seek the Baldrige Award to gain publicity or to "market" the organization as a "quality" firm will find that such aims usually do not withstand the scrutiny that examiners give each applicant.

Perhaps the most dramatic negative example concerns not the Baldrige Award but the Deming Prize (actually, a special version set up recently for non–Japanese organizations). For several years Florida Power & Light worked to prepare to compete. In 1990, FP&L won the Deming Prize for foreign (non–Japanese) organizations. But the efforts expended were so great, says Jeremy Main, writing in *Fortune* magazine,[1] that the company came close to an organizational version of a nervous breakdown.

Main observed that FP&L now has a customer complaint record worse than several other Florida utilities. Earnings have decreased, costs have increased, and FP&L recently announced plans to lay off more than 2000 employees, an action completely out of character for an organization in which TQM is really in operation. (The vice–president for quality was also fired, and the CEO has

---

[1]Jeremy Main, "Is the Baldrige Overblown?" *Fortune*, July 1, 1991. (Pages 62–65.)

been replaced.) One profit center, however, has been the unit that sells consulting services to other organizations interested in TQM. The central feature of their program is a step–by–step problem solving/improvement process called the QI (for quality improvement) way. But when the new CEO spoke with employees he reported widespread resentment. People told him that there was a preoccupation with process and following the steps of the QI way. He said there seemed to be "less recognition for making good business decisions than for following the QI process."

In hindsight it is clear that FP&L went well beyond a reasonable level of effort, partly because the concern from the beginning was less with quality than with winning the Prize. A real danger is the possibility that firms competing for the Baldrige may make the same mistake, forgetting or ignoring the real goal of quality improvement in favor of the short–lived publicity attained by winning the award.

That would represent a terrible waste of resources and energy. In his *Fortune* article Jeremy Main is understandably critical of firms that devote unreasonably great efforts to winning quality awards. But even a "normal" degree of effort is considerable. Most Baldrige Award winners spend several years working on TQM before even applying for the award (and we're talking *real* years here, not total staff time combined and stated as though one person were doing it all). Before winning the Baldrige Award Globe Metallurgical, a relatively small organization, worked for four years to get ready to compete. It took Xerox five years to prepare. Motorola spent seven years.

Not only are a substantial up–front application fee and extensive staff time required, winners are obligated to share with others what they have learned. In 1989 Motorola people made 352 speeches to conventions and corporations, and Motorola responded to over a thousand inquiries from other companies. Senior executives of a small firm like Globe Metallurgical gave speeches in Singapore and Moscow, along with 134 less distant talks.[2]

Houston–based Wallace Company won a 1990 Baldrige. CEO John W. Wallace believes that the cost of the company's efforts to share with others its TQM learnings contributed to the firm's 1991 entry into Chapter 11 bankruptcy.[3] We suspect that misdirected energies, turned toward winning the Baldrige instead of applying TQM, also had something to do with the Wallace Company's problems.

With such cost and effort required, along with the real prospect of economic danger and the low probability of actually winning, why would any organization even want to compete for a Baldrige Award? Winners and losers alike say that working for the Baldrige Award demonstrates in action their absolute commitment to TQM. And, in addition, they report that the most concrete reward is the feedback received.

David Kearns, former CEO of Xerox, says that 90% of the value of the process is in the feedback. David Luther, VP for Quality at Corning — a "loser" — says, "Its the cheapest consulting you can ever get."[4] The feedback received from its 1988 losing effort

---

[2]Jeremy Main, "How to Win the Baldrige Award." *Fortune,* April 23, 1990. (Pages 110–112, 116.)

[3]Robert C. Hill and Sara M. Freedman, "Managing the Quality Process: Lessons from a Baldrige Award Winner." *The Academy of Management Executive,* February 1992. (Pages 76–88.)

[4]Jeremy Main, *op. cit.,* page 112.

helped Milliken & Company to win the Baldrige in 1989. CEO Roger Milliken says, "Applying for the Baldrige and getting the feedback they give you is of incredible value to a company."[5] In sum, it is the feedback that makes the process worthwhile, feedback that tracks the organization's efforts and outcomes and helps to further advance the TQM process.

Some quality experts, including Deming, believe that competing for the Baldrige Award represents misdirected energy and effort. David Snediker, VP for Quality at Battelle, a behavioral science research center in Ohio, argues that firms should be competing for business, not for awards.[6] Despite such examples as provided by FP&L and the Wallace Company, we must express qualified disagreement. That is, if efforts to achieve a Baldrige Award (or a Deming Prize) are part of an organization's active commitment to TQM, the payback can be well worth the cost. If, however, the intent is to win the award, whether to enhance the CEO's ego or to make a good impression with customers, as a "quality oriented" company, then no expense and no amount of effort can be justified.

---

[5]Jeremy Main, *op. cit.*, page 110.

[6]Jeremy Main, *op. cit.*, page 116.

Appendix C

Resources

This brief appendix gives readers who are seriously interested in pursuing TQM some starting points. We will indicate which two or three books are absolute "must read" material, as well as where to go for help (with names and numbers). Major resources are given for each of the three basic aspects of TQM: the tools, customer orientation, and culture.

Tools

Books. The single best resource for publications about TQM tools is the Productivity Press, P.O. Box 3007, Cambridge, MA 02140 (Telephone: 617 497-5146). While their materials tend to be expensive, ranging from $40 for a book on total production maintenance to $3500 for a manual on how to implement a just-in-time manufacturing system, the materials are very current and cover just about every tool imaginable. A good place to start is the *Handbook of Quality Tools* by Kazuo Ozeki and Tetsuichi Asaka. We have mentioned several of the other books published by Productivity Press, in our Endnotes.

Another important publisher in this field is the Industrial Engineering and Management Press, a division of the Institute of Industrial Engineers (a major professional organization). IIE books concentrate more on management's role than on how to use specific quality control tools and techniques. For information and a list of current books, write to IIE, Publication Sales, 25 Technology Park, Norcross, GA 30092, or call (404) 449–0460.

Seminars/Technical Assistance. Productivity Press' parent organization, Productivity, Inc., conducts seminars and provides consultants on TQM. Their toll free information number is 1–800–888–6485. (Address: 101 Merritt 7 Corporate Park, Norwalk, CT 06851; Telephone: 203 846–3777.) The Institute of Industrial Engineers also sponsors seminars and an annual national professional meeting that includes many workshops and seminars; see above for their address or call the telephone number given above.

Another, high quality approach to learning and using tools and techniques is offered by a non–profit organization called GOAL/QPC (Growth Opportunity Alliance of Greater Lawrence/Quality, Productivity, and Competitiveness). Write to GOAL/QPC at 13 Branch Street, Methuen, MA 01844, or phone (508) 685–3900.

Quality for the Customer

Books/Videos. There are any number of books on customer service, but most do not focus on TQM or quality in the sense used here. Some that do, or that approach such a focus are:

> Jay W. Spechler, *When America Does It Right; Case Studies in Service Quality.* Norcross, GA: Industrial Engineering Press, 1988.

> Joseph M. Juran, *Juran on Planning for Quality.* New York: Free Press, 1988.

Larry W. Kennedy, *Quality Management in the Nonprofit World.* San Francisco: Jossey-Bass, 1991.

William H. Davidow and Bro Uttal, *Total Customer Service.* New York: Harper & Row, 1989.

A wide variety of additional, relevant publications by Joseph M. Juran and his associates is available from the Juran Institute, Inc. (Address: 11 River Road, Wilton, CT 06897-0811; Telephone: 203 834-1700; Fax: 203 834-9891.)

For video materials we suggest examining some of the programs available from the Juran Institute. Two films produced by Britannica, Inc., *TQC/Manufacturing* and *TQC/Service*, also give a sound basic introduction to TQM in terms of an integrated "quality for the customer" approach. Another fine video program, *Competing Through Quality,* has been developed by David A. Garvin, Professor of Business Administration at Harvard, available from Nathan/Tyler, 535 Boylston Street, Boston, MA 02116.

Seminars/Technical Assistance. The Juran Institute conducts many public seminars, year-round, in various major cities in the U.S. and abroad. These seminars focus on a systemic approach to managing for total quality, as mentioned in Chapter Three. For information write or call the Juran Institute, Inc. (see above).

TQM Culture

Books/Videos. Not an "easy read," but certainly the most TQM culture-focused book written by any of the recognized experts is Deming's classic *Out of the Crisis* (Cambridge, MA: MIT Center for Advanced Engineering Study, 1986). A more readable exposition of Deming's thought can be found in Mary Walton's book *The Deming Management Method* (New York: Putnam Perigee, 1986), which we have cited often. The most recent Deming–centered book, and one that may be more faithful to the views Deming expresses in *Out of the Crisis,* is Rafael Aguayo's *Dr. Deming: The American Who Taught the Japanese About Quality* (New York: Carol Publishing Group/"A Lyle Stuart Book," 1990). A sense of the nature of TQM culture can be obtained by a careful reading of Tom Peters' *Thriving On Chaos* (New York: Knopf, 1988).

For a definitive view of TQM as a culture change approach, see any or all of the sixteen volumes that comprise *The Deming Library,* available from Films, Inc. In particular we recommend Volume II ("The 14 Points") and Volume X ("How Managers and Workers Can Change").

Seminars/Technical Assistance. W. Edwards Deming still conducts public seminars, some of which are offered through George Washington University in Washington, DC. You can write to Dr. Deming for information, at 4924 Butterworth Place, Washington, DC 20016.

The Center for Creative Leadership has developed a program, "Systems Leadership," focused on the strategies by which top executives use vision to build values relating to quality and excellence into their organizations' culture. For information contact the Center, P.O. Box 26300, 5000 Laurinda Drive, Greensboro, NC 27438–6300, telephone (919) 288–7210.

D. Scott Sink's seminar, "Being a Changemaster in Quality and Productivity Management," incorporates a strong focus on both quality for the customer and the nature of TQM culture. For information, contact the Virginia Productivity Center at Virginia Tech in Blacksburg, telephone (703) 231–4568.

The Center for Value Based Leadership, working with the University of Dayton School of Engineering, conducts a variety of value-centered and culture–focused seminar programs. For information write to The Center, 532 Stonehaven Road, Dayton, OH 45429, or call (513) 298–7783.

Marshall Sashkin & Associates serve as resources to organizations interested in Total Quality Management. Our aims and approach are described in this book: to develop an understanding of how TQM works (in terms of tools, techniques and training); to show why TQM works as an organizational system designed on the basis of quality for the customer; and, most of all, to focus on how organizational leaders can act to create a TQM culture. For further information please call (301) 552–9523 or write to MS&A, P.O. Box 620, Seabrook, Maryland 20703–0620.

Index

Achieving goals 60
Adapting 60
Aguayo, R. 22, 26, 74,
  79, 93, 125, 134, 138,
  142
Appraisals 34
Authority and respon-
  sibility 67

Baldrige Award 11, 68,
  72, 121, 159
Beliefs 59
Bell Canada 63
Bell Labs 57
Benchmarks 74
Bennis, W. 101, 120
Bhote, K. R. 40, 127
Bonus payments 73

Cadillac 106
CEO pay 83
Chaparrel Steel 70
Chrysler Corp. 93
Common causes 16, 39,
  64, 122
Competition 33, 74, 78
Continuous improvement
  17, 25, 27, 28, 29, 41, 63

Control 67
Control Chart 13, 151
Control of people 60, 66
Control of processes 60
Cooperation 53, 74, 135
Cooperation, and
  competition 76, 134, 135
Coordinating 60
Corporate culture 95
Correcting defects, cost
  of 79
Cost reduction 79, 137
Cost, of customer loss
  79, 137
Costs, unknown 79, 137
Covey, S. R. 116, 120
Cross-function team 117
Cultural leadership 96,
  108
Cultural support 8
Cultural symbols 95
Culture 24, 26, 37, 42,
  58, 59, 87, 95, 96, 113,
  134, 135, 143, 171
Culture elements 62
Culture, definition 86
Culture, management of
  27

De Pree, M. 101, 120, 145
Deal, T. E. 95, 96
Deming W. E. 9, 11, 16, 22, 26, 34, 45, 52, 102, 120, 123, 172
Deming Cycle 12
Deming Prize 22
Design for manufacture 57
Drucker, P. 79, 83

Employee involvement 73
Employee ownership 83, 92, 104, 141
Empowerment 67, 88, 92, 100, 131
Enabling 70, 131
Equality 93, 142
Equifinality 116
Equity 92, 93, 142
ESOP 84

Fair pay 92
Fairness 80, 93, 94
Fear 29, 62, 66, 78, 93, 137
Federal Express 65, 68
Feigenbaum, A. V. 35, 46, 127, 128
Fein, M. 72
Fishbone diagram 153

Florida Power & Light 148, 164
Flow chart 156
Ford Motor Co. 48
Ford, H. 60
Fourteen points 27, 32, 125

Gainsharing 72, 132
Garvin, D. A. 46, 124, 128, 171
General Motors 60
Globe Metallurgical 72, 165, 166

Halberstam, D. A. 19, 21, 23, 60, 78, 79
Hawthorne Studies 11, 122
Herman Miller 84, 101, 145
Herzberg, F. 88, 140
Hewlett-Packard 78
Hofstede, G. 73, 134
Hopper, G. 38

IBM 67, 73, 74, 78
Implementing TQM 116
Improshare 72
Inspection 11, 27, 51
International Association of Machinists 145

Ishikawa, I. 21, 24, 124
Ishikawa, K. 24, 35, 124, 127
Ishikawa diagram 153

Japan 5, 20, 22, 78, 108
Job design 78, 88, 91, 100, 140
Job security 78, 93, 136
Johnsonville Foods 68
Judgment vs. improvement 62
Juran, J. M. 22, 23, 24, 35, 38, 45, 58, 77, 118, 126, 128, 171
JUSE 20, 24

Keidanren 21, 124
Kohn, A. 78, 136

Leadership 29, 95, 96, 107, 113, 117
Likert, R. 2
Lower control limit 14

Mackay, H. 51, 84, 129
Maier, N. R. F. 121
Management support 43
Mass inspection 51
Mazda 103, 146
Merit rating 74, 75

MITI 24, 25, 124
Modeling values 100
Motorola 28, 73, 165

New tools 40
Nordstrom's 46
Normal distribution 13, 14, 74

Organizational culture 24
Organizational philosophy 97

Pareto Chart 152
Pareto Principle 52
Participation 10
Participative management 91
Pay equity 82, 83, 92, 138
Pay policies 92
PDCA Cycle 38
Performance appraisal 74
Performance evaluation 33
Peters, T. 68
Philosophy 26, 27, 35
Policies 98
Policy 99, 144
Process metric 64
Procter & Gamble 93, 130

Profit sharing 72, 104,
    132
Program 99, 144
Programs 98

QC 6
QCs 5, 10
Quality checkpoints 49
Quality circles 5
Quality control, defini-
    tion 25
Quality function
    deployment 56
Quality management process
    55
Quality, definitions 45
Quotas 31

Results metric 63
Reward systems 73, 134
Rewards 71, 99, 132, 134
Rewards, individual 71,
    73, 134

Saturn 118, 119, 148
Scanlon Plan 72
Self-managing teams 77,
    90
Seven old tools 38, 151
Shell Canada 106
Shewhart, W. A. 12, 23,
    38, 52, 122

Short-term 32
Sink, D. Scott 55, 130,
    172
Slogans 30, 48, 49
Social tools 87, 94
Socio-technical systems
    77
Special causes 16, 39,
    64, 122
Specifications 15
Staffing 99, 144
Statistical control charts
    12
Statistical process control
    18
Statistical tools 37
Stew Leonard's 46
Suggestion systems 73,
    133
Suppliers 53
Symbolic rewards 106
Symbols 71, 99

Team ethic 78
Teams 90, 118, 147
Techniques 42
The five s's 41
The Reckoning 19, 21,
    23, 60, 78, 79
Tools 37, 169
Total production
    maintenance 41
TQM culture 84, 171,
    172

TQM programs 112
TQM tools 37, 169
TQM, definition 25
Training 17, 118, 148

Unions 97, 102, 145, 146
Upper control limit 14

Values 59, 100, 101
Variability 12, 14
Virginia Fibre 72, 86
Vision 97

Wal–Mart 28, 53, 125
Wallace Co. 69, 131
Walton, M. 20, 21, 26,
    122, 123, 125
Walton, R. E. 77, 118,
    135, 140
Wegmans 46

About the Author

Marshall Sashkin is a senior associate in the Office of Educational Research and Improvement, the U.S. Department of Education's research applications arm, where he helps develop and guide applied research to improve schools. Marshall grew up in Los Angeles and attended the University of California, Los Angeles, receiving a bachelors degree in psychology. He earned his doctorate in organizational psychology from the University of Michigan and has taught at various institutions. From 1979 to 1984 he was a professor of industrial and organizational psychology at the University of Maryland. He is currently an adjunct professor of psychology and administrative sciences at George Washington University.

Marshall has conducted research and published in the areas of leadership, participation, and organizational change. He is the author or co-author of more than ten books and monographs, and fifty research reports. His work has appeared in the *Psychological Review,* the *Journal of Applied Psychology,* the *Academy of Management Review,* and other research publications. For seven years he served as editor of the research and practice journal *Group & Organization Studies* and he is now an assistant editor of the ASTD-sponsored research journal *Human Resource Development Quarterly.*

As a principal partner in Marshall Sashkin & Associates, Marshall has been a consultant to various large organizations, including General Electric, TRW, the Internal Revenue Service, and the World Bank. His work over the past ten years has centered on assessing and improving top-level leadership and he is the author of the widely-used *Leader Behavior Questionnaire (The Visionary Leader).* Marshall's current research and practice focus on leadership, including the measurement of organizational excellence and changing organizational cultures through visionary leadership.

About the Author

Kenneth J. Kiser is an associate professor of sociology at Oklahoma State University and consults widely to top management on issues of quality. Ken is a native of Oklahoma and earned a bachelors in political science and economics and a masters degree in sociology from Oklahoma State. He went on to receive his doctorate in sociology, with a focus on systems analysis, from the Ohio State University.

A consultant to Virginia Fibre Corporation, Bay State Gas Company, the Naval Ship Systems Engineering Station (in Philadelphia), Hillcrest Medical Center (in Tulsa), and many other organizations, Ken has spent more than a decade working with top-level managers to improve quality and organizational performance. His earlier work life includes being a floorman at an open hearth Bethlehem Steel plant and an hourly employee at a Buick Motors Division parts production supply warehouse. Ken has been a member of the United Steelworkers Union and the United Automobile Workers Union.

From 1985 to 1991 Ken was Associate Director of the Virginia Productivity Center. He was also, from 1988 to 1990, a visiting professor in the Department of Industrial and Systems Engineering at Virginia Polytechnic Institute and State University (Virginia Tech).